Rejection Free™
for Life.

Books by Scott Allan

Check out these other bestselling books by Scott Allan. You can visit his website at **www.scottallanauthor.com** to stay up to date on all future book releases, or amazon.com/author/scottallan

Empower Your Thoughts: Control Worry and Anxiety, Develop a Positive Mental Attitude, and Master Your Mindset

Empower Your Fear: Leverage Your Fears To Rise Above Mediocrity and Turn Self-Doubt Into a Confident Plan of Action

Empower Your Success: Success Strategies to Maximize Performance, Take Positive Action, and Engage Your Enthusiasm for Living a Great Life

Rejection Reset: A Strategic Step-By-Step Program for Restoring Self-Confidence, Reshaping an Inferior Mindset, and Thriving In a Shame-Free Lifestyle

Rejection Free: How To Choose Yourself First and Take Charge of Your Life By Confidently Asking For What You Want

Do It Scared: Charge Forward With Confidence, Conquer Resistance, and Break Through Your Limitations

Relaunch Your Life: Break the Cycle of Self-Defeat, Destroy Negative Emotions, and Reclaim Your Personal Power

Drive Your Destiny: Create a Vision for Your Life, Build Better Habits for Wealth and Health, and Unlock Your Inner Greatness

The Discipline of Masters: Destroy Big Obstacles, Master Your Time, Capture Creative Ideas and Become the Leader You Were Born to Be

The Master of Achievement: Conquer Fear and Adversity, Maximize Big Goals, Supercharge Your Success and Develop a Purpose Driven Mindset

Undefeated: Persevere in the Face of Adversity, Master the Art of Never Giving Up, and Always Beat the Odds Stacked Against You

Fail Big: Fail Your Way to Success and Break All the Rules to Get There

Lifestyle Mastery Series: Vol 1: Books 1—3: Drive Your Destiny, The Discipline of Masters, and The Master of Achievement

Rejection Free™
For Life

2-Books-in-1

Book 1: Rejection Reset
Book 2: Rejection Free

Scott Allan

ISBN Paperback: 978-1-989599-70-9

ISBN eBook: 978-1-989599-69-3

ISBN Hardcover: 978-1-989599-75-4

Dedication

For all the brave men and women who struggle with rejection and refuse to be defeated. You are showing the rest of us that our dreams matter.

Keep pushing forward.

CONTENTS

Free Gift

As a way of saying thanks for your purchase, I'm offering a free digital product that's exclusive to readers of the *Rejection Free For Life* series:

The Fearless Confidence Action Guide: 17 Action Plans for Overcoming Fear and Increasing Confidence

To learn more, go to the link below and gain access right now:

https://www.subscribepage.com/o5i3r4

Introduction:
Rejection Free for Life

Welcome to the Rejection Free for Life series. This volume contains both books in the series: *Rejection Reset* and *Rejection Free*. Now, you can enjoy both books combined and, learn through your own *Rejection Free* experience that is shaping thousands of lives across the universe.

Both versions of this book have been revised and updated to enhance your learning experience. Here is an overview of what you will learn in *Rejection Free for Life*:

Rejection Reset

In this book, I will teach you about the cycle of rejection and how it manifests itself through daily repetition of bad habits. You will learn how to identify the triggers and behaviors that perpetuate the cycle of defeat. You will understand why you harbor feelings of inferiority, and develop fearless confidence and take intentional action so you can recover from the pain of social rejection, and start living a more fulfilling lifestyle.

In Rejection Reset, you will discover how to:

- Take immediate action against the fear of rejection so that you can feel great about yourself

- Conquer your pain points of jealousy, inferiority, inadequacy and vulnerability

- Stop trying to measure up to other people and always do your best by being who you really are

- Build healthy social relationships with people and get confident with yourself in social settings

- Implement the 6-step process for creating lasting change and breaking the negative cycle

Rejection Reset is a program full of easy-to-implement steps you can put into action today and see concrete results. You will *learn to identify* the triggers and behaviors that perpetuate the cycle of defeat, understand *why* you feel inferior, and specific *actions you can take* to defeat rejection sensitivity and begin living your best life.

Rejection Free™

Rejection Free teaches you to free yourself from the feelings of shame and the fear of loss. By taking intentional action in the face of fear, you release yourself from an emotional rollercoaster and learn to live your life with greater confidence.

This is a comprehensive guide to help you conquer the fear of rejection through learning how to trust yourself first. By taking deliberate action to free yourself from the feelings of shame and the fear of loss, you can break out of your comfort zone.

In *Rejection Free*, you will learn how to …

- Ask for what you want without the fear of hearing *NO.*
- Stop trying to please the wrong people and pay attention to the right ones.
- Realize that rejection isn't all about you (and how inspiring this is!).
- Put an end to the trap of predictability and the ways it hurts your chances for success.

- Overcome your self-doubt and become great at asking for what you want the most.
- Supercharge your confidence and take charge of your life.

Rejection Free™ will teach you how to turn rejection into your greatest opportunity. You'll discover the best strategies for converting helplessness into a confident plan of action, and gain greater confidence in your personal life and work.

Bonus Material

There is 2 bonus chapters at the back of this book:

- 7 Ways to Overcome Rejection Sensitivity.

- Join the 30-day *Rejected on Purpose* challenge. Become Rejection Free by desensitizing your fears of rejection.

The Rejection Free Journey

I love the topic of rejection and that is why I dedicated my time and expertise into learning everything about this subject. The more I research, the deeper it goes. There are millions of people who suffer from the condition of **self-rejection**. It is a major cause for why we set limitations on who we are and what we can achieve. Ultimately, the level of success you reach is measured by your ability to rewire you' mind for success instead of failure. Your potential is untapped ʳ unlimited!

I want you to know that the word *impossible* is only a realiⁱ mind. The fear of rejection will hold you back indefinitely ʹ face the challenge to become rejection free. Rejection ʳ Self-Rejection are real. They hold you down while y beating.

Your only chance is a system of recovery that tea free. Become *Rejection Free* and live the rest c you love by being who you truly are, breaking through all the mental roadblocks to fulfill your dreams.

You are magnificent and extraordinary, even if you struggle to believe this. We are here to win, and the *Rejection Free* framework is your gateway to building an extraordinary life. I am here to help you, and together, we can defeat the darkness.

For updates on future book releases, and to sign up for my newsletter and receive weekly strategies on creating a freedom-rich lifestyle, visit:

https://scottallanauthor.com

Now, let's dive into these books.

It's time to become **Rejection Free** and challenge the fears holding you back!

"One of life's fundamental truths states, 'Ask and you shall receive.' As kids we get used to asking for things, but somehow, we lose this ability in adulthood. We come up with all sorts of excuses and reasons to avoid any possibility of criticism or rejection.

— **Jack Canfield,** bestselling author of *The Success Principles*

Rejection
Reset

Restore Social Confidence, **Reshape** Your Inferior
Mindset, and **Thrive** in a Shame-Free Lifestyle

Scott Allan

www.scottallanauthor.com

The Pains of Rejection

"You have to build calluses on your brain just like how you build calluses on your hands. Callus your mind through pain and suffering."

— **David Goggins**,
American ultra-marathon runner, triathlete and
author of *Can't Hurt Me*

Have you ever been in a social situation where you felt fearful and too intimidated to speak? Do you believe you have nothing to contribute to a conversation so you keep quiet most of the time? Do you feel rejected around people and feel that nobody sees the "real" you? Are you afraid to express your ideas openly because you might get a verbal put-down?

If this sounds like a familiar story, you are not alone. The fear of rejection is a dilemma that affects everyone to varying degrees: at home, at work, and in society we are continuously at war with criticism, judgment, opinions, and our desire to be accepted.

The Hurts of Rejection

According to researcher Michael Murphy at the University of British Columbia, *"Targeted rejection is central to some of life's most distressing experiences – things like getting broken up with, getting fired, and being excluded from your peer group at school,"* said Murphy, in an article appearing in the *Huffington Post*.

Rejection can be compared to any other illness in that, if it goes untreated, it grows worse. In fact, the rejected person can actually experience intense feelings of emotional and physical pain.

In an article published in the *Michigan News*, a recent study reveals: *"The same regions of the brain that become active in response to painful sensory experiences are activated during intense experiences of social rejection."*

Rejection can cause severe emotional pain, very similar to the pain we experience when we are physically injured. For example, being excluded from a party when everyone else you know gets invited, suddenly being dumped in a relationship, or being treated as if we don't matter. All of these can cause depression, headaches and elicit psychological fear.

The University of Michigan social psychologist, Ethan Kross states in the Proceedings of the National Academy of Sciences:

"On the surface, spilling a hot cup of coffee on yourself and thinking about how rejected you feel when you look at the picture of a person that you recently experienced an unwanted break-up with may seem to elicit very different types of pain. But this research shows that they may be even more similar than initially thought."

Psychologist and author Guy Winch, Ph.D., states that, "Many times rejection does 50% of the damage and we do the other 50%." What he is referring to is that when we get rejected, we begin with a stream of negative self-talk that spirals into a form of self-rejection, and, in some cases, self-hatred for oneself.

This negative self-talk could stem from any situation in which we experience rejection from a romantic relationship, a co-worker, or friend who ignores us in passing. Your emotions turn into a hypersensitive radar that starts to see rejection everywhere.

Guy Winch also states in his book, *Emotional First Aid*, "Rejections elicit emotional pain so sharp it affects our thinking, floods us with anger, erodes our confidence and self-esteem, and destabilizes our fundamental feeling of belonging."

Social rejection is one of the biggest self-defeating behaviors that affects millions of people both at home and at work. In their daily lives most people are not aware they are making critical choices and taking actions detrimental to their social life.

The problem is that most people who live with this affliction cling to an "emotional ledge" most of their lives. They hang on while expecting help to arrive. But it does not. Living a life of quiet desperation, the cycle of self-defeat brought about by rejection becomes seemingly impossible to break.

Many get frustrated and want a quick fix to end their pain, so they turn to addictions and bad habits to numb the negative emotions taking hold of their lives. They want to escape from feeling inferior. They want to avoid those thoughts and feelings feeding into their distilled beliefs of inadequacy. They want to be in control of their lives but they just don't know how to get to that stage.

Hypersensitivity to rejection plays a role in the success or failure of each of us. The more sensitive we are, the less empowered we feel.

Using various escape strategies, such as addiction or other negative coping mechanisms, may work in the short run. In the long term, it sets people up for failure. That rescue boat they keep hoping for never arrives and they are left alone, abandoned, and clinging for help.

There are many excuses people use to justify staying stuck in these situations. Those excuses become lies that bury the truth and keep them spinning in place. If this is you, I say it is time to do something about this. You can change the way things are. You can start right now. You can make the right choices to free yourself.

This is where *Rejection Reset* can help you.

The Purpose of *Rejection Reset*

Just like you, I know what it is like to go through life with low self-esteem and a total lack of confidence. In time, this feeds into disempowering beliefs and negative thoughts that can create heavy self-doubt. I know what it is like to struggle with personal and business relationships when your fear is the deciding factor that influences key decisions.

I know the feeling of always having to compensate for inadequacies that appear real when around certain people or social situations. It is not fun when you are always sitting on edge, waiting for someone to finally figure out the darkest secret you want to keep hidden.

Feeling like "loners" and that nobody understands us, we take to hiding behind false personas and massive egos to protect our shame-based selves. This way of life keeps us functioning below our real potential and prevents us from creating genuine relationships, especially with ourselves.

As we will see later, shame is at the core of our inferior self. We feel flawed and defective somehow. Feeling helpless to cope with these feelings because they are a part of us, and living in isolation as well as fearing that someone is going to find out our "big secret," we have built up a showcase of coping strategies to protect ourselves from harm.

My purpose and mission are to help you work through your feelings of inferiority and self-doubt. I want you to live an energized lifestyle and to develop the real skills for facing the challenges that life imposes so you can enjoy the outstanding life that you deserve.

I wrote this book not from the objective viewpoint of someone like a psychotherapist, but from the personal viewpoint of someone who has struggled with what you are experiencing.

Scott Allan: a Brief Intro

My name is Scott Allan. I am an author, rejection-free confidence coach, and personal development trainer. My books have helped thousands of people just like you to recover from the obstacles that defeat them. My mission is to provide you with the tools, life skills, and confidence to take control of your life.

I have struggled with failure and self-defeat for most of my life. Through addictions, negative behaviors, and a life of struggling to change bad habits, I have worked to overcome many obstacles on my journey toward freedom. So, just like you, I know what it is like to struggle and feel like you are spinning your wheels. I know what it is like to feel completely alone on the journey.

I know that change is not easy. If you have nobody giving you advice or guiding you along the way, it is easier to give in to the lesser path. I do not want you to give up; you deserve the best in life, and if you work on yourself just a little bit every day, you can experience the full benefits of what I am going to teach you. So do not wait. The time to take massive action is today.

Even if you have a strong desire to break your limitations, this will not happen until you disengage the core negativities that are keeping you stuck. Thanks to the techniques I am going to share with you in this book, you can begin to live the life that you have always dreamt of but could never quite reach.

You see, if we are not in charge of our lives, someone or something else is. If we are not making choices that empower us, we are making choices that limit us.

If you are grappling with negative emotions and thoughts that keep you stuck, and you want to break free, then you are in the right place. I cannot claim to have all the answers. But, I can tell you that the ideas and strategies in this book come from my own personal experiences, and what I found that helped me get through a lot of the past stuff that was controlling my life. I have made a lot of progress because of the wisdom and teachings past mentors shared with me. I want to share this wisdom with you now.

Why *Rejection Reset* is a Good Fit for You

Rejection Reset is for anyone looking to overcome the hurdles and challenges of dealing with social rejection. The rejection "pain" can take place within your mind [self-rejection] and out there in the real world.

This is a program full of easy-to-implement steps that you can begin to put into action right away and see real results. You will learn how to identify the triggers and behaviors that perpetuate the cycle of defeat, learn why you feel inferior to everyone else, and develop the confidence to take action so you can start to live a more fulfilling lifestyle.

You will learn how to:

- Take immediate action against the fear of rejection so that you can feel great about yourself again

- Conquer your painful points of jealousy, inferiority, inadequacy and vulnerability

- Stop trying to measure up to other people and just be who you are

- Break the mindset of the rejectionist and replace it with healthy, positive habits that focus on creating the life you have always wanted

- Disengage the faulty negative beliefs that kill your motivation and productivity

- Implement powerful strategies that work to replace the worn-out techniques that only serve to defeat you

- Build healthy social relationships with people and get confident with yourself in social settings

- Implement the 6-step process for creating lasting change and breaking the negative cycle

- Practice twelve daily habits and build a new routine to keep you from slipping back into a lifeless rut

Later on, we will look at the coping strategies people use to survive through life when they don't know any other way. I can show you how to create new methods so that you are no longer running away but are taking a stand that empowers the real you. You do not have to just survive anymore; you can learn to live and be yourself.

In this book, I will talk about the cycle of rejection and how it manifests itself through daily repetition of bad habits. I have written this material to be short and concise. There will be no long psychobabble explanations or psychotherapy exercises to probe into the last twenty years of your life and relive painful issues of the past. By the time you have finished reading this book, you will have displaced the rejectionist mindset.

If you're ready, let's dive into chapter 1. You'll learn seven action steps you can take right away to start moving towards a rejection free state of mind.

Chapter 1

Gearing Up for Full Engagement

"Most fears of rejection rest on the desire for approval from other people. Don't base your self-esteem on their opinions."

— **Harvey Mackay**

It is recommended that you put yourself into a clear frame of mind before reading. Induce a relaxed state by focusing on your thoughts and breathing. If you have any negative thoughts that creep into your mind during the next chapter, try to push them away and focus on your positive attributes. We are here to learn and to heal.

Six Strategies You Can Practice Today

As we begin, I want to give you six strategies to put into practice as you read through this book.

1. Be Good to Yourself

One of the biggest hang-ups that defeat many people is the habit of beating up on themselves. They continuously repeat negative thoughts to themselves like "I am not worthy of love," "I am no good," or "I have nothing of value to give to anyone."

They do this through reinforcing conditional behaviors that defeat their actions. By beating themselves up through negative self-talk and harsh criticism, they minimize their personal value by buying into the "I'm worthless" mindset.

This is the great lie that perpetuates itself and grows stronger over the years. The more we repeat these negative messages to ourselves, the more real they become. This has to end if we are to expand beyond our current state.

What I want you to do is give yourself a break here. You are not perfect, but by reading this book you have taken a positive step by making a clear decision to improve yourself.

You could be hard on yourself because somebody else was hard on you. It is time to step up and start being good to yourself. Later on, I will show you the strategies for dealing with nasty negatives. You'll learn how to turn words of self-defeat and limited thoughts into empowering positives that create long-term growth and change.

2. Observe Your Reactions

Starting today, observe how you react to challenging situations. How do you feel around people you think are better than you? What thoughts are going through your mind that devalues your self-worth? When do you feel irritated? Angry? Fearful? Rejected?

This observation is an important step. For now, you don't have to figure anything out. Just watch how you react. You will start to see a pattern develop that you have not noticed before.

Reactions are conditioned behaviors that take the place of common sense and wisdom. By starting to notice your reactions now, you can develop better ways to handle situations that used to baffle you.

Overreacting, or reacting out of fear, is a coping strategy when we feel powerless to deal with difficult situations. We will get into some techniques in the following chapters on how to handle our reactive state so that we can develop a proactive position instead of just letting everything get to us.

3. Focus on Progress, Not Perfection

Perfectionism is a good thing sometimes. It can push us toward greatness instead of settling for mediocrity. It can also be an obstacle that gets in the way of making steady progress in our lives. Afraid of making mistakes, we try to do everything perfectly the first time to avoid failing. In the end we end up stalling and put off taking any kind of action.

We have a strong tendency to do things perfectly or not at all. When reading through this material, put aside the perfectionist and focus on progress that moves you ahead one step at a time. Five things done well are better than one thing done perfectly (and it is never perfect anyway).

Perfectionism is a lie that keeps you stuck. So step back and take it easy. Give yourself space to grow. Allow yourself to make mistakes. I am not perfect; you are not perfect. But you can be perfectly okay.

4. Keep an Open Mind

In this book, I ask that you have an open mind to the ideas and thoughts I am going to share with you. You do not have to accept everything, and not everything may apply to you. But when you are working through this and something suddenly clicks or stops you in your tracks, it could be a sign that something needs more attention.

Focus on the areas of your life that need adjustments. Work to replace what you have to so that you can move forward with your life. Keep in mind that you can create the lifestyle you want. You are not inadequate or flawed, as you may have been led to believe. Keep reminding yourself that you are an exceptional human being and you deserve the best.

Get into the habit of talking to yourself every morning before you leave the house. Practice having this silent conversation with yourself several times a day for relaxation. Focus on calming the voices inside your head that ramble on without meaning. By keeping an open mind, you will feel more relaxed and focused, and this will help you to deal with everyday situations that you find difficult.

5. Give Yourself Time to Heal

I do not want you to get overwhelmed with the process. Personal growth is a work in progress. Your success takes a series of small steps over a period of time. It is not the size of the jump you make that counts, but the number of steps you take along the way. There is no rush. Steady persistence is the key.

This is important, because if you are anything like I was, you will end up quitting soon, as I did many times in the past. I started something, expecting to have amazing results in a week. But when I was not completely transformed I gave up. I started to look for the next quick solution. This led back to my old self-defeating behaviors that worked in the short term because they were reliable.

Just remember, there are no quick fixes. By taking action just a little bit every day, you will build up a powerful reservoir of confidence, self-esteem, and discipline. Take things slowly and give yourself room to explore.

6. Visualize Your New Outcome.

Start to think about what you want to do with your life. Imagine yourself overcoming rejection and feelings of inferiority. See yourself doing, being, and having what you once only dreamt about. You can start to do this right now. Get focused and look at where you are today.

If you are in a bad place emotionally, then that is where you are. It is okay. Everyone has to start from somewhere. We do not have to wait for a perfect moment or the right circumstances to begin; just start from where you are at. The journey ahead of you is unfolding, as it needs to.

Lao Tzu said, "A journey of 1,000 miles begins with a single step." I want you to think of every day from now on as the next step and focus on the goal you are moving toward.

Do not look back and wish that things had been different. They will never be different. You can start to look at the situation differently. Think of every day as a new beginning full of opportunities. What happened yesterday or ten years ago is in the past. This does not mean you should just pretend nothing happened, but know that you are not the only one with a past that was not perfect. What you do today is what matters.

Visualize the life that you have always wanted to have, and not the one you feel stuck with. Visualize yourself doing, being, and living the best possible way you can. Start to think deeply about the direction in which you are now heading. Imagine where you could be in two years, five years, and ten years down the road by committing to a plan of action. The reality you can imagine is the life you can have, if you really want it.

You can choose your own way right now. You can stand up and say no more. You can set your own standards for living instead of the self-imposed limitations that were thrown onto you.

Do not put your life on hold anymore; it is time to make a serious shift in the way you think, feel, and take action.

Chapter Recap

In this chapter, I gave you six actions you can take:

1. **Stop beating yourself up**: Be aware of the reinforcing conditional behaviors that defeat your positive actions. Don't buy into the idea that you are worthless because you are afraid. Everyone is afraid. It is how we deal with it that matters.

2. **Observe your reactions**: How do you react to challenging situations? Do you try to avoid them or run away? By starting to notice your reactions now, you can develop better ways to handle tough situations.

3. **Focus on progress, not perfection**: We are not here to be perfect. We just want to make improvements in how we live our lives and live without hiding. Don't let your fears fail you.

4. **Keep an open mind**: Focus on the areas of your life that need adjustments and work to replace what you have to so that you can move forward with your life.

5. **Give yourself time to heal**: There are no quick fixes. By taking action just a little bit every day, you will build up a powerful reservoir of confidence, self-esteem, and discipline.

6. **Visualize your new outcome**: See yourself where you want to be in one, five, or twenty years from now. Use that mental image as a goal to strive for.

We have a lot to cover so let's not waste any time.

Are you ready?

Turn to the next page and let's begin.

Rejection Truths and Disengaging Critical Negativity

"Shame is the most powerful, master emotion. It's the fear that we're not good enough."

— **Brene Brown,** author of
The Gift of Imperfection

Do you remember the last time that you were rejected by someone? Was it a romantic rejection? Were you rejected in a social group? Did the bank refuse your loan? A group of friends had a night out and you're the only one who didn't get an invitation—and you found out after they posted a group photo to Facebook?

Regardless of how it happened, I think we can agree that rejection is a painful experience. It can cause depression, anxiety, and, in many cases, mental health issues as well as physical symptoms.

According to a study in the Journal Proceedings of the National Academy of Sciences, the experience of rejection can do intense physical harm to the extent that our brain **releases opioids** to combat this pain.

But how do we stop from getting rejected? How do we reduce the chances of rejection? How do we avoid rejection?

These are legitimate questions people have asked me over the years. I will answer these questions in the rest of the book and give you solid strategies to implement as you deal with rejection in a more proactive and logical approach.

The Path of the Rejectionist

Here are five truths about rejection that we will get out into the open right now, before we get on with the rest of the book. Understanding these simple truths will help you to be realistic about rejection and give you greater perspective in dealing with it.

Truth #1: You will experience rejection many times throughout your life.

If you have never been rejected, you have never really tried anything challenging or risky. Rejection belongs to those people who tried and were turned down. By avoiding rejection, we place ourselves in a worse situation: the circumstances of never getting what we truly want.

You may be clever in dodging the perils of rejection, but you'll end up on the rocks just the same. This book is a guide to teach you, not how to avoid rejection, but, on the contrary, how to handle it when it does happen. Notice I said "when" and not "if." You have to accept rejection as a part of everyday life. It is also a critical formula for success.

Truth #2: The solution is internal, not external.

It is easy to think rejection is all about other people pushing us away. But actually, your reaction to rejection is most of the battle. It is how we view ourselves when we are rejected that sets the stage for what comes next.

Was I rejected because of something I did, a flaw that I have, or some hidden character defect that everyone but me can see? One of the core truths is that our internal thoughts and beliefs are deciding factors when we interpret a rejection experience.

Was I turned down because I am no good, or the other person just has no need for what I am offering right now? When we analyze our own internal feelings and thoughts, we can uncover the critical beast that lives there. It is the child that was harshly criticized, the young adult that shied away for lack of confidence around people, or the shame of expressing oneself.

Truth #3: People will judge, but they are not a jury.

People say things all the time. They complain about each other, they express dissatisfaction, and ultimately, when they cannot resolve a situation to their benefit, they will judge and condemn the other by pointing the finger.

As a rejectionist, we take this very personally. What if someone doesn't like me? What do I do? How can I gain their acceptance? How can I set this straight?

Before you try to patch up a big hole, analyze the situation for a moment. The people who judge: are they perfect? Have they been blessed with anything that you haven't?

When you take the time to think with an open mind about the opinions of other people, you may realize that they are judging the world based on:

1. a belief system.

2. a point of view that is not 100 percent accurate.

3. a fear-based mind.

We tend to be hurt by the opinions and judgments of others. Their words and actions, directed against us in a negative way, switch on our rejection sensitivity. This creates stress, fear, and anger. But the truth is, most of the time the opinions of people are based on inaccurate facts.

A point of view is just that—an imperfect opinion. Remember this: most people react out of fear, which leads them to faulty conclusions. Don't build your emotions on illogical claims.

Truth #4: You have nothing to lose.

We try to protect what we are afraid of letting go. We cover what we don't want to lose. Is it any wonder why we are so fearful? Can you imagine what you would gain if you let go of the fear of loss? My guess is, you would get everything you've ever wanted—and then some. But we try to protect ourselves too much. We put up defenses and ready the walls against certain attack. If they want what you have, they'll have to scale your emotions to get it.

There is nothing to lose if you have nothing to lose. When you spend all of your efforts to protect yourself against being injured, you are reinforcing the fears of rejection that are making you fearful.

Allowing yourself a certain level of vulnerability is a good thing. People who recover from rejection recognize that allowing people to see them as they are, while it does increase your chances of being emotionally injured, is the best way to start growing internally. Later on we will look at the ways vulnerability can open up doors for you instead of keeping them closed.

Truth #5: Your past is not your future.

If a child is raised in a family that is emotionally absent, critical, or dysfunctional, these will undoubtedly be passed down to the child. Your shame-based self and the fear of rejection started early. It did for me, too. But it doesn't have to continue.

Your past is not the future unless you decide that it is. In this case, you will continue to play out the same failed reactions, habits, and behaviors you have learned early in life. We can stop this behavior from today.

Over the years, we create coping mechanisms and escape strategies (more on this later) and we make our way into the world full of fear, doubt, low confidence and low self-esteem. The injured child is what we left behind. It is a child who wanted unconditional love and acceptance but never got it. However, we can give this to ourselves; we can be good parents to our inner child.

This recovery is a process, and there are no quick-fix solutions. But you can have success and begin to build your life, creating a new mindset and set of beliefs that work to dig you out of a rut and put you on the right track to having greater confidence and life-fulfilling experiences.

Your Response to Rejection

When something happens to trigger your feelings of rejection, we go through a series of painful emotions. The first instinct is to avoid or flee from the person or situation that is causing this distress.

To defend ourselves against the situations and people who could reject us, we chose to avoid rejection at all costs. We became negative and pessimistic toward any kind of rejection. This negativity morphs into a hypersensitive condition where we start to see rejection everywhere.

The rejection factor, as time progresses, molds itself into a self-fulfilling prophecy. Your core beliefs, accepted long ago by the subconscious as being real, act as the blueprints for all future experiences. In the case of someone who suffers from rejectionism and the need for approval, every action you take, every decision made, is in alignment with your emotions, beliefs, and thoughts.

If this were based on the core strategies of your rejectionism, you would be choosing a path that leads to bad results. For example, this can be something that makes you inadvertently sabotage your efforts, or an addiction that you cannot give up because the rewards are too tempting.

The result is that you create a life built on a weak foundation. Over time the fear manifests itself into a full-blown phobia. This tremendous fear leads to further isolation, poor choices, and emotional dysfunction on many levels. You may have created a system by which you sabotage your success in work or relationships because you know, deep down that it isn't going to work out anyway.

Your life, and the future ahead of you, plays out as a self-fulfilling prophecy. Your thoughts lead to actions that build on choices based on the fear of rejection. The thoughts you develop will manifest into reality. When negative emotions take over and, you run your life from the foundations of a negative base, you can only expect more of the same.

When you are raised as a child to think less of yourself, to believe in your fears, and to stay out of sight and out of mind, those characteristics grow to define you as an adult. You will then operate from a place of unworthiness. Driven by your negative beliefs that you are not worth very much and that everyone is better than you, a flawed reality merges into your existence.

This feeling of unworthiness is the great lie that we are going to expose and dissolve. You have been living a lie. It is an illusion of the worst kind where you believe that at the very core, you are born different. You are different, and so, you learn to stay out of sight. In other words, you act as if you do not exist.

We can change that here. In the following chapters of this book I have outlined a program for you to put into action. By the time you are finished you will be able to deal with rejection, handle anything that comes your way, and push forward no matter what fears you are grappling with.

Chapter Recap

Using rejection truths to disengage critical negativity all starts with you. The fear of rejection, the need to be accepted, and the lengths that we will go to achieve this acceptance are remarkable.

Remember: there are things you can control in life. And there are many things you cannot. We have to distinguish what it is you have power over. Is it other people's emotions, attitudes, opinions, and moods? No. We have no control over any of this. Yet, we allow ourselves to be governed by the attitudes and approval of others. This erroneous governance is how we become sensitive to rejection. By allowing ourselves to reject who we are, it makes it easier for others to reject us as well.

Imagine how your life would change if you learned to control your response to fear, rejection, and criticism? Can you visualize the switch in direction your thoughts would take? The increase in contacts and relationships you could build? How little stress you would have and the ability to let negativity just roll away from you, because you know that you are the creator of your own internal voice?

You would be able to change everything and anything at will.

In the next chapter I will introduce you to the hypersensitive rejectionist and what it means to live with "rejection expectation." You will learn to become a better social conversationalist and communicator—not just with other people, but also with yourself.

Chapter 3

The Hypersensitive Rejectionist and Rejection Expectation

*"Nobody can make you feel inferior
without your consent."*

— **Eleanor Roosevelt**

One of the defining characteristics of someone who struggles with rejection hypersensitivity is that you come to expect rejection as an automatic response to nearly every situation. It is a combination of low self-esteem, confidence, and a host of negative beliefs that point to one thing: I am not worthy. I am inferior to everyone around me.

When you meet someone for the first time you put on an air of confidence that serves to protect you during the interaction. One reason most rejectionists fail at developing strong, long-term relationships is because most interactions are designed on purpose by the rejectionist to be short term.

You avoid any deep or involving relationships if it can be helped. Why do we do this? It takes a lot of energy to appear confident and fearless. Inside you do not feel normal, and your subconscious has been programmed to tell the truth. The reasoning behind this strategy is to, "get out while you can" before they find out just how dull and boring you really are.

Dealing with Rejection Expectation

Rejection expectation is an emotionally painful situation. It keeps you isolated, because the pain of being rejected is so great that it is better to be alone where nobody can get to you. When you expect people to not like you because you just don't fit in, this expectation becomes a self-fulfilling prophecy.

You are awkward and uncomfortable around others. You keep conversations short and time spent with one person at a minimum. During conversations you may suddenly go quiet and appear to the other person as disinterested and detached. They start looking for somebody else to converse with, leaving you "at the table" so to speak.

When you see that same person laughing and having a good time with others because they could not be with you, it reinforces the false truth that you already believe to be true: You are unworthy and incapable of forming new relationships.

Bonding with people is an uphill battle for people dealing with rejection issues. We are always on guard, fighting our inner demons for dominance over a fragile mind. It is a vicious cycle of perpetual self-rejection. Other people have nothing to do with it. We might tag them as the problem, but in fact, you are at war with your own beliefs and insecurities.

Everything you are feeling, all those negative emotions that create anxiety and panic when socializing, are self-made fears that you have created. Somebody else may have planted the seed ages ago, such as a critical parent or guardian, but throughout the years the seed has been taken care of by the master gardener: **You.**

When we can accept responsibility and own our feelings, everything changes. You gain a greater sense of self-control. You raise your confidence level right away. You become a better communicator because you remove your thoughts from concern over what other people are thinking. It is this obsession with, "what will they think?" that perpetuates the rejection cycle.

Socializing and meeting new people is just one form of rejection expectation. Rejection expectation takes place in:

- Job interviews ["I know they won't hire me because I don't have what it takes."]

- Romantic relationships [She'll dump me as soon as she finds someone better."]

- Social situations/Out in public ["You see, they just ignored me and walked right by."]

- Applying for a loan at the bank ["What's the point in applying? They always turn me down, anyway."]

- College applications ["They won't take me. My grades aren't good enough to get in. Besides, I was never good at studying in school].

- Asking for something ["Why bother asking, he will just say, 'NO,' again. People are always refusing my requests."]

This fear is so deep that rejectionists will even avoid filling out an application form for fear of being turned down. When you hear NO, it fulfills the expectations that what you feared was true all along: "I'm not good enough to have this thing." This compounds the embedded belief that *I will always be at the lower rung of the ladder, picking up the scraps that nobody else wanted.*

When you live this way, change becomes an impossibility. It can form into a stagnant routine that, although you may not be completely comfortable with it, will keep you stuck in the same place [an unhealthy relationship, a bad workplace] because the reality of going through the rejection phase repeatedly is too painful. It becomes a lose-lose situation: "Damned if you do and damned if you don't!"

Talking Down to Yourself: The "Voices" of Damnation

As we will see later on, your subconscious mind has been programmed from an early age to believe, develop habits, and talk to you in ways that either support you or destroy you. These messages come at you from deep down under. These are buried under years of conditioning and life experiences that molded the person you are today.

Take a moment to sit relaxed and comfortably. Just let yourself go and relax your mind. Let go of your thoughts. Do not force your thinking in any other way; let whatever thoughts you have flow through you without trying to change them. Then just let them go.

By observing the thought patterns you create—consciously or unconsciously—you can see the patterns of rejection and the process your emotions and correlated thought patterns play out in times of crisis.

In my own personal observations, what I noticed after stepping out of myself is that, when confronted with a situation that I can feel rejection creeping in, there is an internal dialogue that starts up. Those feelings of isolation, loneliness, and that urge to flee, are underlying beliefs that what is happening is real and it is all my fault.

There is an internal dialogue that starts up: "You are the reason people will not like you. There is something wrong with you that separates you from everyone else."

It is this same feeling every time that takes place no matter where you are, and because it is so repetitive, it must be true. Years of conditioning have not been kind.

In the end, there can only be one conclusion:

Nobody rejects you any harsher than you reject yourself.

For most of us, the rejection phase begins long before you enter the room, meet someone new, or give that awe-inspiring speech you have spent weeks preparing for. While it is true some people do not care for you and may even think you are boring, this does not make it universally so.

If someone doesn't like you, it might hurt a little; but if you have those same feelings toward yourself, this can turn into real suffering. We have to relearn how to be kind to ourselves, and to shut down those voices that insult, criticize and condemn. That is not who you are but the voices of a mind still attached to past events. We have a strong tendency to repeat painful experiences that occurred, even decades past, because we haven't truly let them go.

The imagination of a rejected person is a powerful force. While it keeps the victim separated and alone for protection, the imagination lives out its true desires: To be one with the crowd, to go anywhere and be anyone, to be known and famous and loved. But reality eventually comes crashing back in.

We know that we want so much but because fear runs deep, we hold ourselves back from asking for anything. We are forever on the outside wanting it all but too scared to take that leap forward.

If you are reading this book and have made it this far, it is because you can relate to at least a few of the situations here. Now, we need to take action to change, and it has to be a set of proven principles applied repetitively to bring you from that stage of nothingness to one of greatness.

You could be a different person on the inside by next week. You could be acting differently, talking differently, and even working in a different profession. That is, if you desire to take the steps to get you there. If you stay committed and dedicate a part of your day toward recovering, you will start to gradually feel good. Then, good will become great and in time, you will become extraordinary.

Going on the Defensive

Overly sensitive people tend to get defensive when they feel attacked or criticized. In many cases what is mistaken as an attack on character could simply be prodding fun, or someone making an innocent joke. In other situations, it could be an evaluation at work or, you are being blamed for something that isn't your fault.

Whatever the case, the reaction is to take a stand and counterattack the blame. But this can do more damage than good. People who fight back tend to lash out at times without provocation. You might think that you just had to do it when, in fact, the other person meant no real harm.

The other example is when you are being ostracized or criticized; it could be that a co-worker or your boss has just gone off the deep end and you happened to be in the way. Often a counterattack may be more aggressive than the actual attack in the first place. After, you might feel ashamed or embarrassed that you had reacted so strongly, and once you do, you cannot take it back.

Taking a defensive stance puts you on edge. You are constantly ready to fight back and win the argument. I have done this and felt pretty horrible after realizing that the other person wasn't acting aggressively or trying to be critical. It was all in my own head, and I had built it up that he or she had it coming anyway. In the end I only ended up hurting myself.

There is a lot to say for exercising cautious self-control. I know it is not easy but, being defensive acts like a built-in mechanism. You learned to act this way from childhood in response to pain or being rejected.

Now, in adulthood, you revolt against any kind of critical comment, even when it is constructive. Even worse is that it drives people away from you and makes them overly cautious when approaching you about something.

People with hypersensitivity struggle in work-related environments that involve teamwork or communicating with people of authority. It is always "the other guy who did it" and so, unable to see beyond blaming everyone else around them, they reject any proposal for improvement.

Here are three action steps to push you beyond hypersensitivity and develop a resilient mindset. You will become less sensitive and more active in your approach towards others. Focus on one strategy at a time. Move into the next tactic when you are feeling ready.

1. Identify your assumptions. More often than not we are guessing what people think about us. Most of our assumptions are based on fears that stem from past experiences. If we were rejected in the past, people will continue to throw rejection after rejection at us. It becomes an endless loop of personal negativity we throw at ourselves. But it goes without saying that, what you expect from the world is what you will get.

We attract the things that we assume are true. If you walk into a room and you 'assume' that people are going to ignore you or leave you out of the conversation that is what you will see in very interaction. You will actually look for it and when you find it, you will be able to confirm your assumptions as coming true.

So let's come back to reality. Take a moment to observe the assumptions you have about yourself and the world around you. Ask yourself, "Is this assumption I have true, or is it just my own fear talking? Do people really think this about me?"

When we identify the assumptions that we have, it puts things in perspective. In most cases, hypersensitivity is all about how we think the world perceives us. The cure to this is not to focus on how others view you but on how you view yourself. Do you feel confident? Are your thoughts in alignment with the person you want to be? Are you tearing yourself down, or expecting someone else to do it?

Once you have tagged your false assumptions, you can work on dismissing them. We have a strong tendency to reject ourselves before anyone else can. This is like giving the world permission to do so. The moment you stop rejecting yourself, the world will no longer matter.

What other people think, judge or assume about you will not matter, because your confidence is not built on the opinions of others. It can only come from within you. Remember what I discussed earlier: we are not basing our recovery from rejection on the opinions of the world but how we think and feel about ourselves.

2. Don't accept everything someone says as the truth. People are right sometimes...and wrong more times than they are right. Just because someone doesn't agree with you doesn't make him or her right. Also, just because everyone agrees with you doesn't mean that you have no flaws. Not all criticism is valid, so this is why we need to step back and evaluate what is being said.

People can be wrong in their opinions but we can find a good message in the harshest of critics at times. Open your mind up to the possibilities and stay fixed on seeing the truth. If you are not sure if what is being said is the truth, try asking someone. A close friend or colleague will often be more honest if you ask them.

3. Take it now, work it out later. One of the pitfalls of dealing with our sensitivity is that we are always on edge. We are ready to defend ourselves at any moment. When a critic jumps in and says something derogatory or critiques our performance at work, we are ready with teeth bared. But what if there is some truth to what they say? What if what we perceive as criticism is really an effort to help us out?

If you are sensitive to criticism, as many people are, you have your ego on alert and your pride is ready to take action. But remember that anything you say in the heat of the moment will be remembered.

Suggested action: take the remarks or criticism people give you and take time to reflect on what has been said. If someone made a comment about your report, read the paper over again to look for areas of improvement. There are people who will complain about you and are unhappy with an action you took, work you did, or the way you handled a certain situation.

The rule of thumb is, take it now but work through it later. Take time to reflect on their feedback. Look for ways you could use that feedback to improve your relationship with others and make better improvements in your own life.

Chapter Recap

It takes great patience to be kind to yourself. If you are sensitive to rejection, it hurts. Consider that the emotional pain isn't necessarily coming from the other person but from within yourself. We beat up on ourselves when we don't get it right, or when we think we fail to please someone else. To get beyond our over-sensitivity requires us to be diligent with our actions.

This attention to our own reactions means when you come across a critical person, remember that they might have a lesson to teach us. If not, you can decide to listen to what was said or brush it aside.

Don't mistake good criticism for complaining. A complainer has nothing to add. They have one goal and that is to tear down another so they can feel justified in their arguments. You can sweep this aside. If someone complains about you when you aren't around and you catch wind of it, confront that person. They may deny they said anything but at least you know there isn't any validation to anything they say.

In the next chapter we will get into **predictable choices** and what it means to make choices based on the fear we are experiencing in the moment.

Chapter 4

Making Predictable Choices

"It is impossible for you to be angry and laugh at the same time. Anger and laughter are mutually exclusive and you have the power to choose either."

— **Wayne Dyer**, bestselling author of
The Power of Intention

Rejection is a painful experience when we don't have the tools or strategies to deal with it effectively. Without proper support or guidance, you can spend your life fending off critics and staying below the rejection radar so as to avoid dealing with the pain of being told NO, or just ignored altogether.

When you are living in a place of constant fear such as the fear of being rejected or the fear of meeting people, it directly affects the quality of the choices you make.

Here is an example: Let's say you wanted to work in a new field that would be more in line with your goals, but that industry requires you to engage with people and get very personal. An example of this would be a sales position. You might avoid that kind of job, even if you really want it, because of the social pressure you feel of putting yourself out there where dealing with rejection is a part of the job.

Likewise, having a fear of job interviews you decide to stay in the same line of work, not because you want to, but because you need to avoid getting rejected in an interview. For years I stayed stuck in a job because of this. I had anxiety when I even typed up my resume. The jobs I wanted had certain requirements that I didn't have so I avoided them. Excuses like: "Oh, I'm sure they have already found somebody else," or, "I am too old to work there now anyway." The excuse was my escape tactic to keep me away from actually taking action.

Choosing the Predictable Pathway

When you operate from that place of fear, you choose the predictable pathway. Predictable situations, even if they are painful, are comfortable and we feel that we are in more control of the outcome.

By trying to control fear, we end up creating a level of anxiety that keeps us stuck in emotional pain. By escaping into our place of comfort, what we think of as a safety net is really a cage. You will never grow or expand beyond your fear when you choose to stay scared.

Here is another example. A girl named Sally wants to approach Jeff to ask him out. But Jeff intimidates her because he is popular, well educated, and seems very confident of himself. Sally hesitates and, even though she has had several chances to approach him, she has anxiety and fears that he will say "NO."

She starts to make excuses:

- *"I'm too busy for dating anyways."*
- *"I'm sure he has a girlfriend or he is probably married."*
- *"I'll approach him when I've lost more weight."*
- *"I'll wait until he notices me first."*

The excuses validate the behavior and sway our choices. You can then take the predictable path without feeling any shame or fear of the other person saying no. Sally will then find someone that is either at the same level as her or beneath her somehow. She is never fulfilled in the relationships she settles for, but she can feel comfortable in the situation knowing there is less risk in rejection.

These situations have a common theme. Both people made choices that keep them stuck at the same level. They never do anything to better themselves or go after the job, the relationship, or the life that they really want.

If your choices are based out of fear of looking silly, failing, or being turned down, you choose the predictable path that is safe. You can't lose. There is no risk involved. You might think you are winning out, but let's face it, you will never get what you want. You will spend the rest of your days envious of the people who have what they want, and wishing you could be more like that.

In the end, people settle for what they can get or whoever will have them, instead of going for what they could have if they just pushed past the pain threshold of vulnerability.

The same can be said for the work we do. Did you know that over half the people employed are unhappy in their work? If so many people don't want to be at the place they are working, why do they stay? Many people stay stuck because of the belief that they won't get anything better. Others would rather stay in a job they don't like than have to go through the rejection of interviews.

So what happens is, we take what we can get so we don't have to face that inevitable rejection letter.

When we settle for second best, we might position our worth at the bottom of the scale. You may take a job you can get instead of one that you really wanted because of the chance they would refuse you. You get into a relationship with someone who treats you badly, but you don't leave because your self-esteem has convinced you that this is what you deserve. You could spend your life settling for anything that you can get instead of what you really want, or deserve.

Now, what if you could change this right now? What if, instead of settling for second best or just anything that comes your way, you choose to go after what you want instead of what you can get. Instead of settling, you raise the bar and decide right now to live by a set of new standards. Instead of going for what is easy, you go for what is right. Instead of giving into comfort and playing it safe, you will take a little risk and feel okay with it.

How different would your life be if you approached the subject of rejection from another angle? We know that getting rejected is something we can't avoid. It is a part of life. The people who embrace it as a necessary obstacle are the people that reach the summit, while everyone else is stuck at the base of the mountain, clambering for a foothold on a difficult climb.

The act of being rejected has power only when we feed it. By this, I mean if you accept everything that you don't want, you'll be left with the unwanted scraps that nobody else needed.

Your choices right now will open up a different door for you to walk through. You can change your satisfaction, fulfillment, and confidence levels the moment you make a higher choice for yourself, as soon as you decide that you will take the high road for a change.

What is a decision you could make right now that would prompt you to move in a new direction? How about raising your standards? Make a change to your personal value system?

Many times, we want to change but we stick with the same standards that get us nowhere. Stuck in jobs we don't like, relationships that make us sick, or living in an area that isn't suitable.

While it is important to choose what we want in life, it is equally important to identify with what we don't want.

Raise Your Standards

When you make an intentional decision on the things that you will no longer tolerate, from yourself and others, it changes everything. You could remove your core rejection issues overnight if you made a decision about what you deemed acceptable.

In most cases, we lower our values and thus lower our personal standards just so we can fit in. It is a form of people pleasing: you accept whatever people throw at you because you believe that is what you're worth.

By raising standards across the board, you find yourself making higher-level decisions that bring you greater opportunity. Would you feel sensitive if someone ignored you if your standards were raised? You'd think, "Fine, I'll find someone better." You can shift your entire perspective right now, today, by making a conscious decision on what you will no longer accept.

Will you let someone talk down to you without standing up for yourself?

Will you accept criticism from yourself if you don't succeed?

Will you continue to allow yourself to believe that you are unworthy or unlovable?

Right now, you are going to make a list of the beliefs, behaviors and attitudes that you no longer accept. This list has two parts.

1. What I no longer accept from myself.

2. What I no longer accept from other people.

You can divide your list up into the various areas of your life such as relationships, work, friends, personal values, and social situations.

Once you can identify what you don't want, you can focus on what you do want. For example, if someone you know treats you badly, set the standards for what you will accept from this person. Be honest with them. Call them out when they put you down or act inappropriately. If they don't change, you can leave.

Take intentional action when something goes against your raised standards. For whatever it's worth, do not lower your standards to please someone else. If you do, you'll be back where you started.

Chapter Recap

Look for moments in your day-to-day life that you choose to do something out of fear. Did you agree to do something for fear of being frowned on? Were you intimidated to speak for fear of being ridiculed? Rejection is a cycle that can hold us back. Instead of being our true selves, we hide in the shadows from shame.

Look for the good in rejection. There is an upside to rejection that we often fail to see. Instead of a villain that we should avoid, think of it as a necessary companion always there to help you move forward, even if this means progress is painful.

Be aware of how you react to the moods of others. When they are angry or being overly controlling or demanding, is your fear on high alert? Are you ready to agree with anything they say just to get along? If you are overly sensitive to the environment when it is hostile, you may try to 'get along' to avoid being targeted. But if this is the case, you'll always resort to people-pleasing.

In the end, we want to base our choices in life, not out of fear but by asking ourselves this one question: "Am I taking action based on my values? Is this the right thing to do?"

Dealing with rejection is a learning curve. Take it head on and embrace the lesson it has to teach.

Moving into the next chapter we will learn about shifting the negative beliefs so we can deal with our feelings of inferiority and destroy limited thinking patterns.

Chapter 5

Shifting Negative Beliefs

"If you don't have solid beliefs, you cannot build a stable life. Beliefs are like the foundation of a building, and they are the foundation to build your life upon."

— **Alfred A. Montapert**

In this chapter, I am going to cover the limiting beliefs you may have about yourself and how to convert these to positive beliefs. We can accomplish this in five simple steps that I'll cover later.

The core of an inferiority mindset begins with the negative beliefs that have damaged a person's self-esteem and devalued their worth. In order to be free and build a life of better quality, making a shift in just one of our beliefs can have tremendous impact on our emotions and thoughts.

When you disengage the beliefs keeping you trapped, it frees up space for healthier beliefs to create a new operating system. As long as our limiting beliefs convince us that something is wrong with us, the negative cycle continues to repeat itself.

This negativity cycling is how we stay stuck: By re-living the same behaviors and focusing on damaging, worn-out thoughts day in and day out. When we focus on replacing our faulty beliefs, we can start to shift away from the inferiority persona and move towards building a more positive outlook.

Belief Limitations Exposed

Negative core beliefs express lies about who we are and what we can do. These are supported by a thousand distorted thoughts and corrupt ideas working together to support the false statements we have come to believe in.

Whereas destructive beliefs can ruin us, a system of positive beliefs focused on building confidence will generate a system of healthier thoughts and boost our self-esteem and confidence.

Negative beliefs are the cracks in character that need to be mended if any kind of long-term success is to be achieved. The causes of these beliefs extend into past childhood events as well as life experiences that we linked our pain to.

For example, if you experienced rejection as a child from a parent per se, you may have formed the internal beliefs that you are unlovable and therefore not worthy of love or acceptance. This conditioned belief also lends to hypersensitivity, as we covered in the previous chapter.

Remember:

Your beliefs have had a lifetime to grow and form deep roots within your conscious and subconscious mind.

While directing our lives based on the false perception of our past reality, we limit our chances for any kind of real growth or personal development. But it is not necessary to go back and dig up all of our old skeletons.

We can start from where we are today. Regardless of how a belief was created or why, we can focus on the NOW. The past is not your future. How you perceive an event makes it a lesson learned or a painful experience you choose not to repeat.

You can implement five steps to reverse the way you have been thinking, believing, and behaving. You can change these beliefs to work for you instead of against you. The goal here is to identify and discard the beliefs you have that don't support you, while shifting towards a set of new beliefs to empower your life.

Many of your beliefs about yourself are lies that have been reinforced since childhood. Once we integrate a belief we rarely question it but come to accept it as the way things are.

By choosing to develop more empowering beliefs that support and build the way of life you desire to have, you can create a detailed map for success that guides you to the places you wish to go. You are creating your reality, as you want it, instead of just passively accepting the way things are.

Whatever your current state is, you can change that in an instant. Earlier we talked about raising your standards so that the rejection you have been sensitive to can no longer hurt you. By deciding what we will no longer take, and then deciding what is acceptable, we can shift the beliefs that are managing our current state.

The Six-Step Process for Changing a Belief

You can pull yourself out of the current state you're in if you don't want to be there. You can shift your emotions to be positive and create more optimism in your life. With this in mind, a chosen system of thoughts that empower you also leads to the development of an empowering belief system.

Step 1: Identify the belief you want to change. Identifying the beliefs you want to change is the first step to taking positive action and doing something about it. You can only change something if you know what you need to change and why you want to change it.

Core negative beliefs that are making you feel inferior, inadequate, and worthless should be first on your list. Why hang on to your painful thoughts any longer? This is a tough step for most people. We have been feeding into our pain for so long it starts to appear normal.

I can assure you that in working through your pain, and recognizing the negative beliefs you created about yourself, your life starts to take a dramatic shift.

Here are some examples of the beliefs you may have about yourself. See if you recognize any of these:

"Everything bad that happens to me is my fault."

"I feel like I am less competent than everybody else when it comes to success or getting ahead in life."

"I feel like a failure or a 'nobody' when in the presence of other people who are obviously better than me."

"I have no qualities worth talking about that anyone would be interested in."

"I should be perfect at all times. I have to show people I am perfect."

"I am inherently flawed."

"I am inferior to everyone else. They are smarter, more educated, and seem to land on their feet when all I do is fail from day to day."

"I'm no good, and everybody knows it."

"Once someone gets to know me, they will just leave me like everybody else."

"My family was extremely dysfunctional; so, I am dysfunctional."

"If only she would stop treating me that way, I'd feel better about this situation and myself."

You might have a number of faulty beliefs about yourself that have disempowered you throughout most of your life. I know I did before I worked to turn them around. The key is to recognize what they are. Some are buried deep. Others are more noticeable and are running through your mind on automatic pilot a hundred times a day. They feel so normal that you do not question their validity.

Take time to write them out and list as many as you can. You can start with parts of the short list above that apply and add to it with your own negative beliefs. Pay attention to the beliefs that target your self-esteem and devalue your worth.

Step 2: Disempower the old belief by injecting doubt and uncertainty. In this next step you want to inject doubt and uncertainty into the equation. It is time to take a stand and question your belief thoroughly, analyzing it under a mental microscope through strict analysis. It is time to put your beliefs on trial.

You are going to question your beliefs, attacking their vulnerability, tearing down their walls, and weakening their structure. If a belief has been built on lies and falsehoods, it will not stand up to the scrutiny of your attack.

Here is an example:

"My family was extremely dysfunctional; so, I am dysfunctional."

Using this as an example, let's take a look. Begin by questioning this belief. Act as if you are actually interrogating this belief. Talk back to it; talk down to it. Take away its power. Make a decision to reject this as any truth.

Here is an example of what I wrote:

"What is the basis for this belief?"

"My family life was not perfect by any means. My parents loved me conditionally and they had their own issues to deal with. Many times I felt rejected or outcast. But this does not mean that I am dysfunctional. To a degree, isn't everyone? Don't we all struggle with our own defects? I refuse to accept this belief anymore."

Go deep with your ideas and push back hard. Then, ask pertinent questions that disengage the power your belief has over you. Put your belief on trial! Tell yourself that this is not a reality you choose to believe in anymore. Disown it completely. Choose to believe in something else. This decision to have a new belief is when your mind makes a shift towards reframing what it has been trained to accept.

Step 3: Reframe the new belief while discarding the old one. When reframing a new belief, the key is to convince ourselves it is real. We have to believe it! This is difficult to do when we start out.

Full of fear, self-doubt, and lacking in confidence, we can easily fall back into old patterns of defeat. We can convince ourselves that the negative belief (I am no good because I always fail, so why bother) is true.

When you decide to replace your old beliefs, you are making a firm commitment: *I refuse to feel this way anymore. From now on I am going to believe this about myself and reject all negative thoughts that try to enter my mind.* If you do this enough over the course of days and weeks to come you will be thinking and behaving differently.

Now...

Step 4: Visualize the person you will become once you have created that new belief. Visualize yourself behaving differently. Visualize taking new and decisive actions, and pushing through your fear instead of being blocked by it. See yourself overcoming your inferiority complex by living life in a more vigorous way.

Step 5: Reinforce the new belief, taking further repetitive action toward making it real. Now that you have a solid idea of the changes you want, start by supporting your new belief. Take immediate action and reframe your old belief with the new one.

If you tear down the old belief but do nothing to replace it, when difficult times come up (and they will) you will resort to that old destructive way of thinking again. When this happens, just remember what your replacement belief is and continue to reinforce it over and over. Such reinforcement has to be done consistently in order to succeed.

One way to take intentional action on this is to write out ten of your favorite quotes. Utilize the power of positive words. From there you can move onto positive affirmations. Repeat these several times a day. It will be uncomfortable at first, but be persistent.

The more you use words of positive power, the faster you can shift your beliefs to accepting what you are saying and thinking. Persistence and consistency are the keys. Keep at it. Soon you will be able to pull out your positive mental toolbox and use it to overpower those negative thoughts and words that punish.

Self-conversation is a powerful tool. Your negative beliefs used this tool against you for many years. Now you know that you can choose thoughts that support your new belief. Give your new belief lots of encouragement and support. Repeat it as many times as you need to. Convince yourself that it is true!

Step 6: Follow Up Action. In this final stage, you are going to continually strengthen your belief through convincing evidence. You will also alter your actions and behaviors to align with the new belief as it starts to plant its roots deep into your subconscious.

A belief responds to action and confirmation that what it is experiencing through your thoughts and actions is your reality.

It is important to follow up your reinforcement of the new beliefs on a continual basis. Create the beliefs you want to have. Do not settle on or accept the thoughts that devalue you.

Once a year, you could give yourself a small test to see where you are at with your beliefs and, analyze whether they are consistent with your desires and purpose.

You may discover, as I have, that there are new discrepancies with your current beliefs and values. If so, you can always update your belief system every year, making subtle changes here and there, adjusting your course in order to stay on track.

Keep Track of Your Empowering Beliefs

We have a lot of faulty beliefs about ourselves. I am referring to those beliefs that do not accurately represent who we are. We buy into these false messages because our belief system has been conditioned and tricked into thinking this is real, and this is who I am.

Buying in to these inaccurate beliefs is false conditioning. We must observe our behavior and the thoughts and beliefs that are driving it. The beliefs that feed us those negative messages sound like truths, but they are the lies we must replace.

I recommend that you keep track of both **empowering** and **disempowering** beliefs in a notebook. On one side, write down the beliefs that you want to change; these are your disempowering beliefs. On the other side, write down the positive beliefs that empower you.

An example of a disempowering belief would be:

"I'll never succeed at this. I'll always be poor because I can't save money."

An empowering belief, however, could be:

"I can earn as much money as I want when I build the business I have been dreaming of."

Negative beliefs keep you stuck, and hold you back from pushing forward. Positive beliefs build up your self-esteem and confidence.

They stimulate your mind to snap to action and get unstuck. Work to focus on the beliefs that are helping you to succeed.

We should take some time out to observe what we are thinking. The best time for this is when we find ourselves in a situation when we feel rejected. This could be when our confidence is challenged, someone is criticizing us, or we feel the urge to counterattack.

Chapter Recap

We have just looked at the limiting beliefs that formed our rejectionist mindset. Disengage these beliefs and we are well on our way to defeating any situation where you feel inferior or that your personal worth is being scrutinized. Be patient and give it time.

As I suggested, make lists of both negative and positive beliefs. Read them both out loud. Cross out the disempowering beliefs and focus on the positive ones. Use positive quotes and affirmations to support positive thinking and action, and work them into framing a new mindset.

Now, let's move into the next chapter right away because I am going to cover the cycle of rejection. I will show you the process and pattern that starts working when you are in a situation that causes you to feel inferior.

Chapter 6

The Cycle of Rejection

"People tend to dwell more on negative things than on good things. So the mind then becomes obsessed with negative things, with judgments, guilt and anxiety produced by thoughts about the future and so on."

— Eckhart Tolle

In the last chapter you gained some good insight on how to change negative beliefs about yourself. Now, I am going to show you the cycle that accompanies the rejection mindset.

This is the painful pattern of defeat that has been formed over years of conditioning. In this chapter I will go through each of the stages to give you a clear idea what happens when you choose to be rejected in any situation.

The condition of feeling inferior and inadequate can be best explained in the cycle that keeps the condition active. Our goal, as you will see in this book, is to deactivate the cycle you are currently using and then replace it with a healthier cycle.

Why Change is Difficult

Change is difficult because people do the same things over and over again expecting different results. Einstein and other philosophers once described this as, "the definition of insanity."

If you want a different result, you have to do things in a different manner than you have been doing them. This includes habit change or shifting your beliefs and thoughts to react and behave differently than before.

Einstein also said: *"You can't solve a problem at the same level that it was created."*

Frustration sets in when you have the desire to make a change, such as to stop acting out in ways that reinforces your negative behavior, but the same feelings of inadequacy continue to prevail when we engage in the same behavior that keeps us in a rut.

For change to be successful, you have to reframe your reality. This new reality is going to be your new constructive pattern to replace the old destructive one. Instead of acting out the old ways, you are going to replace these with new healthy behaviors that move you away from the old you. It is not easy, but I can show you a way that worked for many others and me.

Basically, the cycle of defeat that we create when our sense of rejection is triggered looks like this:

1. An internal trigger is "switched on" by external events or conditions.

2. A pain point is activated.

3. A faulty choice is made based on previous experience.

4. An escape tactic or coping mechanism is initiated.

5. There is a result that has a favorable outcome/conclusion.

6. The cycle is repeated, or the result, such as escaping from our pain, is achieved and a faulty conclusion is reached.

Breaking Down the Steps

An internal trigger is switched on: When you experience a situation that is stressful and causes anxiety or fear, a trigger is activated by an external event. Trigger activation could be brought on by familiar situations connected to childhood trauma or circumstances that trigger feelings of loneliness, depression, or anger.

The resulting action could be to act out defensively or engage in compulsive behavior to minimize the internal pain. The trigger is what happens first; the action you choose to deal with it is selected by the nature of the pain point experienced.

A pain point is activated: I will talk about pain points in more detail shortly. The initial trigger that sets us off activates our various pain points. In most cases it is driven by the shame-based persona.

Pain points can be feelings of vulnerability, defectiveness, rejection, failure, or abandonment that act as our primary switch and determine what we will do next. A pain point is experienced when a situation comes up that triggers stress, anxiety or fear. Based on this, we choose a self-defeating behavior to cope with the situation.

A faulty choice is made based on previous experience: We choose to behave or respond using a technique that masks the pain. Who wants to feel those things when we can hide or control it using a coping strategy?

When choices are made by default, they are performed automatically without thought or analysis of the conclusions that we end up with. It is our default choice. At the time, we might think we have no other choice, but we do. We convince ourselves we have no other options so that we have an excuse to act out without taking responsibility for the consequences.

There is real power in our choices when we decide with a mind that is fully switched on. When we fall back on default choices, we give up our power to take charge and just let things happen to us instead of taking control. Responsibility only comes to those who have earned it.

A technique is chosen based on either escape or coping strategy: Once a pain point has been activated we have to choose an avoidance technique; this is a coping strategy that enables us to deal with the situation by choosing an action that works to eliminate or numb out fear and anxiety. The type of and degree of behavior chosen depends on the level of pain or discomfort you feel.

We can counterattack and defend, possibly by using an addiction such as alcohol, sex, or binge eating. Or, we might turn into a critical monster and start tearing someone down as soon as they are not around. Escape tactics and coping strategies focus on short-term solutions that eventually fail. They have a goal to help us escape but really, the end result is further denial and isolation.

Expected outcome relieves tension, frustration, or stress; a conclusion is drawn that proves our faulty beliefs.

After applying the coping strategy that focuses on escaping or avoidance, the predicted outcome results and tension and anxiety are relieved at least until the next trigger.

And then...

The cycle reinforces and repeats.

During the rejection cycle a pattern is followed that leads to a repetition of damaging choices, which solidifies the behavior. In a situation in which we feel vulnerable, fearful, or totally defective, the obvious choice is to either cope with it or escape from it.

This pattern is the core of our coping strategy, and it keeps our negative beliefs, emotions, and thoughts working to support our false reality. This reality is an illusion that we continue to buy into.

Failure Expectation and the Escape Plan

When the 'fear of rejection' switch is triggered, there is an automatic reaction to deal with the emotional pain that's coming. This switch could be triggered by the fear of a job interview, talking to people we are attracted to, or public speaking.

Whatever the situation is, there is a level of anxiety experienced. It is this initial nervousness that starts the process and we then buy into a certain falsehood associated with the situation or event.

We begin to visualize what could happen if our voice cracks or we lose confidence. We see ourselves failing and feel others watching us and judging. All of these fears build up. We then enter the situation, expecting to be rejected, judged, or looked down on at some level. In other words, we are expecting the failure we know is coming. By choosing this expectation at an unconscious level we manifest the failure or rejection.

The purpose of this cycle is avoidance and escape. Rather than cope with a situation we are not prepared to handle, we choose the default path. It is the only option when we believe that nothing else exists, and that there is no other way out.

Let's say our escape route is an addiction such as drinking or eating junk food. When we have stress or pressure brought on by a situation that we decide we cannot face up to or control, our pain point is activated and fear-based thoughts choose the path of least resistance (an addiction) to cope with the situation.

When we feed into the action by either filling up on junk food or wanting to get drunk, we escape the pain of facing reality. This has a good conclusion based on a distorted reality.

You see, this cycle is self-defeating, yet we recreate it and tap into it whenever a fear-based situation or problem comes up. The reaction is to "get out of the house before it burns down."

Many people had to deal with some painful emotions as a child when they were abandoned, felt inadequate, or were criticized. Having no say in this, they formed a coping mechanism that molded into the only way out for them.

The **escape plan** is the way out; it is their back door to a survival mechanism that promised to relive the emotional pain. In reality, it becomes a box that keeps them trapped. For many people, they spend decades locked in this turbulent cycle that has no end.

We are going to work at shifting your perception so that you see yourself through a different lens. Imagine if you were to look through a telescope on one end and then turn it around and look through the other end. The view is different.

Your aim is to shift your view of the world. You have to set your own expectations so that you do not fall victim to a cycle of defeat. Your goal is to break the pattern of reacting to the pain point by engaging in healthy techniques that diminish anxiety and fear through healthy choices.

Now, there are two paths we can take when dealing with diminishing fear and anxiety. One path is the escape plan. Our pain point is triggered; we want to avoid pain, so, by natural default, our habit is to activate a technique (defeat strategy) to deal with pain reduction.

The selected addiction path looks like the best choice, but, in reality, it is the path to failure. We may experience the momentary relief of evading the fear and pain but, in the end, it just drives us into further seclusion. An example would be an addiction or faulty behavior such as lying, exaggerating, or trying to impress others.

The other path, the positive self-talk one, is the path of courage. It is the goal we are going to achieve here. When we take this high road, we feel the fear and push through it anyway instead of taking the easy way and fleeing.

We are willing to feel what is happening. Instead of choosing by default, we take the way out of the pain by choosing a healthier way of responding. This is the conscious choice. The way to be courageous is to do the thing that you fear the most. Take action when you are afraid.

A cycle is only broken when different choices are made followed by a new course of action. The reward you get from going through the grit is far more fulfilling than sticking to what has always worked and what has always failed you.

Learned Behavior & Framed Reality

Nobody is born inadequate or flawed. Character defects are a part of life, but when we act out using strategies to control our defects, we make them stronger.

In the case of rejectionism, our aim in the "Cycle of Defeat," is to avoid feeling rejected. There are several ways we can do this. For example: criticizing others before they get to us, retaliate by destroying someone else's reputation, or isolating ourselves from a group to get away from the risk of looking stupid or being exposed.

The bottom line is shame: We are afraid that someone is going to find out our dirty little secret and then the party is over. Our ego will do anything to prevent this.

As a child we may have been injured in some way; we had no defense. As an adult living in the big world, everything is exposed for the world to see. But at our core, that injured child still seeks retribution; it wants an apology or nothing at all.

We have framed our reality around protecting this child. It is a fear-based reality, but it demands our attention at all times. We are on guard constantly. And, when we keep a close vigil to protect what is ours, the Cycle of Defeat becomes our strategy. Now we are going to work at changing this strategy and replacing it with a new one.

The new cycle is designed to replace the old one, almost how we would switch out the parts in a car. It can be done, and the process is similar. We have seen the cycle that plays out when a situation or individual threatens our ego.

In order to cope with the threat, action has to be taken; this action, up to this point, has been a negative cycle of defeat that led to a favorable result that reduced anxiety or made us feel less uncomfortable. But it is a faulty system based on escape. We are not dealing with anything; we are sweeping the problem under the rug.

Chapter Recap

Be aware of your internal triggers. When you experience a situation that is stressful and causes anxiety or fear, a trigger is activated by an external event.

Pain points, such as feelings of vulnerability, defectiveness, rejection, failure, or abandonment, act as our primary switch and determine what we will do next.

We use various coping strategies, such as counterattacking, to deal with our unresolved issues to mask the pain.

A faulty choice is made based on previous experience: We choose to behave or respond using a technique that masks the pain.

We can respond to your rejection in two ways: Fight or flee. We can escape or take courage and do something about it. A cycle is only broken when different choices are made followed by a new course of action.

You can change by framing a new reality for yourself.

Chapter 7

The Breakthrough Cycle

"Between stimulus and response there is a space. In that space is our power to choose our response. In our response lies our growth and our freedom."

— **Victor E. Frankl,** Auschwitz survivor and author of
Man's Search for Meaning

With some simple strategies and solutions you can learn to confront your inner demons. You can develop greater courage to talk to them, push them out of the way, and charge forward without being held back.

Our goal is to disempower the beliefs that are slowing you down and keeping you stuck, because in the end, that is all they are: **obstacles**. They are not permanent barriers, but they do rob you of your personal power over time if not treated.

As we will see, you can choose to engage in the empowering thoughts, actions and behaviors that serve you best. You can rise above the barriers of personal self-defeat and tap into that inner strength that you know is there.

Making Choices That Matter

Let's take a look at making choices. When we find ourselves in a situation that threatens our self-esteem, or could expose us to shame, a survival mechanism kicks in. We unconsciously make a decision to take action to prevent exposing our pain point.

Our thoughts, wired into this cycle, are fearful like animals that flee from fire. Our thoughts are directed toward self-preservation. We will do anything to avoid being humiliated or have our flaws exposed. Seeing our flaws under a "social microscope" is one of our big fears.

When it comes to making an empowering choice, we choose poorly. That is to say, we choose the path that alleviates the pain. This is usually a coping strategy that has been tested again and again, and based on the reward gained from using this strategy, this appears to be the logical choice.

One technique, or "escape strategy plan," is to engage in some behavior that forces you to make a choice. This choice is made, in most cases, through acting out and just letting it happen passively. We need to be intentional about our choices if they are to have any long-term impact.

Think about a choice you have made in the past that was made with intention. How did you come to make it? Was it based on relevant information? Did you make the choice after considering other options? Was the choice successful or did it lead to a bad result?

Choices based on intentional effort have a high probability of achieving a successful outcome. When you choose unconsciously (without any logical thinking or reasoning), you have little to do with controlling the outcome, and in making a decision based on your fearful emotions you end up taking a lower path that you will later regret. This eventually becomes a repetitive cycle that we fall into.

This can occur through a psychological process known as repetition compulsion, where we unconsciously repeat the same painful experiences over and over again. If being rejected and feeling like "a nobody" is a normal experience, it could become natural to continue reliving this same experience over and over.

Breaking the Cycle

In everything you do there are choices. If you choose path A, you will get that. Choose path B, you get something else [will you take the red pill or the blue one?]. Sometimes what you might get is a surprise you were least expecting, but if you keep doing the same thing over and over, the surprise turns to expectation based on the result and conclusion of previous "experiments."

Like a bad habit that delivers the same outcome, there is no surprise left. We know what to expect from engaging in the same behaviors repeatedly. This is why we need a new set of actions to create a better cycle. Over the years we may have developed a pattern of bad results that continue to reinforce the cycle of defeat that feeds into the inferiority complex.

You can end this all right now.

Instead of feeling worthless, you decide your worthiness. Instead of rejecting yourself, learn to love yourself and all your faults. Instead of comparing yourself to other people who have more, try to see life as an abundant opportunity. Up until now, you have been living with less; now we are going to focus on building abundance and a higher quality lifestyle through six simple steps.

The Six-Step Process for Creating Lasting Change

Here is the six-step process you can implement right away and start to see immediate results.

1. Identify the behavior you want to change. Admitting that you are not perfect is a big step. When you admit that something in your life is not working, you set the stage to make it work.

Here is an example: After taking time to observe my behavior, I knew that one of my character defects was trying to impress others. I would brag about things I was working on, made myself sound smarter and more confident, and implied that I had big things going on. I wanted people who had what I wanted to recognize me as an equal. I was seeking validation and acceptance. If I did not get it, I would feel rejected and worthless.

Looking for external validation from others could be setting yourself up for a let-down. Your sense of value is riding on their opinions, most of which are not based on facts, but driven by emotions. A person's perception of you can, and will, change from day to day. The only true validation you need is your own.

Seeing this was a major breakthrough. When I admitted that this behavior was driving people away and not drawing them to me, I caught myself in the pattern. I could actually see when I was trying to impress others. Gradually, by stopping this behavior before it happened, I reduced the amount of times I did this. This allowed me to be honest, forthcoming, and more down-to-earth.

2. Make a decision today to change this behavior. Until you decide what it is you want, nothing happens. If you say, "Someday, I'll get around to it," that day will come five years later, and you will still be stuck.

Make a decision right now and stick with it. Choose to have a different outcome. Believe in what you have yet to discover. Turn your actions into conscious choices instead of actions based on default that inevitably lead to failure tearing away at your self-esteem and confidence.

Making this decision is something you have to reinforce again and again. Make your decision to focus on small changes every day. Keep at it and do not give up. Make a decision—everyday—that you are going to overcome any obstacle that stands in your way. This includes your limited beliefs, doubts, and fears that crop up.

3. Decide what you are willing to do to change. What are you willing to do? What will you have to give up in order to successfully implement these changes? What old behaviors are you struggling to let go of? What will be the price you pay if you do not make concessions?

These are important questions. There are many times when people want to change something (a bad habit or an obstacle) but, when it comes to paying the price, they start to negotiate. They want to change, but they soon realize nothing comes for free. To have the one thing we really desire usually requires surrendering something else. The things you insist on holding on to could be the same vices keeping you trapped.

When you are ready to pay the price in full, you will. By letting go gradually you can have everything you have ever wanted: peace of mind, stronger relationships, and a healthier frame of mind.

4. Choose a new response and action. What action is needed to implement changes right now? Is it a shift in your attitude? An addiction you are holding onto? Letting go of your attachment to a negative behavior? When you become willing to do whatever it takes, when you go all in with a full commitment to paying the price, your resistance towards creating new behavior loses its power and is broken down.

The reason most people struggle is because they are holding on too tight while still uncertain if they want to pay that price. But what does this mean? What are you going to pay? More importantly, what are you willing to give up?

Do you want to change your feelings of inferiority but still criticize others because it feels good or empowers you? Will you give up your defensiveness or keep it because you never know when you are going to need it?

Whenever you feel stuck and you are looking for a way to get out, remember that change always follows action. When you take intentional action towards your objectives you condition yourself to fear less and do more.

You may make mistakes, but nobody ever failed who put in an honest effort to push ahead and make a situation better. By staying focused on what you really want and by working continuously on improving your situation, you are taking a first step toward something much bigger.

5. Be ready for setbacks. It is important to be realistic. Nothing comes easily and more often than not you have to try at something several times before it works. This is the reason why, when you experience a setback or fall back into old patterns of defeat, it is important that you don't beat yourself up.

Not everything happens according to plan. What matters is that we have a good idea of the direction we want to take. Only then can we intentionally decide the right course of action to move towards that goal.

6. Continue to repeat and reinforce your success. This system works best when you take immediate action, recognize what is working best, and analyze the results you got so you can continue to fine-tune your strategy. If you do not succeed right away, keep working at it and continually reinforce your positive habits.

Repeat those positive actions that bring about the desired outcome and put an end to the behaviors that are dragging you down. After putting this cycle into practice, you will be able to recognize clearly how to act instead of react, how to choose instead of letting it happen by default, and how to be yourself instead of living a lie.

This is the essence of gaining freedom: When you are empowering your life by choice, learning by trial and error, doing what works, and eliminating the rest.

Chapter Recap

Now that you know how to use the new cycle to create change, be sure to implement it when your issues with rejection are challenged.

Always remember that nobody can reject you. Only you can do it to yourself. And now that you have the know-how to take action, there is nothing stopping you.

When I started to implement positive strategies into my life I could sense the *self-saboteur* within wanting to take back control. After repeating the positive cycle that begins with a conscious choice to get well, the negative side that wanted to ruin it all faded away.

When I experienced those feelings of inferiority I chose not to believe it. In choosing, you become empowered. And when this happens, any other barrier that stands in your way collapses.

Chapter 8

The Social Trigger Response

"Every time I thought I was being rejected from something good, I was actually being re-directed to something better."

— **Dr. Steve Maraboli**

A trigger response is a person, place, or situation that kicks our fear of rejection into taking action and reacting [out of fear] to a fearful situation. We feel compelled to act out in a destructive way. This is done by using an escape tactic to deal with a painful or fearful moment. Before we decide on the escape tactic to use, there has to be something happening that will trigger you to react.

Activating Trigger Responses

So, what is a trigger response? It is what sends an alcoholic back to drinking when seeing people having a good time in a bar. It is when a smoker will return to the habit when engaged in a situation where people are smoking.

It is when a social situation triggers feelings of shame when someone points out one of your flaws. It is when pressure in a social environment could trigger your rejectionist fears and trigger you to feel anxious or suddenly lose all confidence.

Our trigger responses could be activated by any one of the following situations:

- *Meeting people for the first time.*

- *Negative thoughts or "bad" thinking.*

- *Revisiting memory spots from your past.*

- *A situation that triggers a painful past experience.*

- *Hanging around with people who have more than you do, such as money, popularity, a nice car, or a family.*

- *Exposure to an addiction that once had fulfilling rewards.*

- *A demanding relationship.*

- *An overpowering boss or someone who demeans or criticizes you.*

Any one of these trigger points could cause you to react. Our triggers are defense mechanisms designed to protect us. Or so we are led to believe. But what they really function as is low-level trigger points. Instead of seeking a higher end solution, we buy into the easy path that usually turns into an escape route.

Emotional triggers are danger points because they rob us of all our hard work. Maybe you spent weeks or months trying to get through your emotional baggage, and then, wham! Next thing you know, you are confronted with a situation that compels you to act out. This makes you take action on something you'll later regret.

Remember that nobody can set us off. I often hear people complain that he or she really "set me off" or "my boss really gets on my nerves". But did they really? Are we not in control of our own emotions? Is someone forcing us to feel this way?

We are in control of our own emotional state at all times. Nobody can make us feel or do anything without our permission. It just seems that way when we lose control and convince ourselves we have no choice and so, we resort to taking negative action to get back at those people who are out to get us.

The Trigger and Emotion

The trigger is what sets us off, the switch is the emotion that it triggers (defensiveness, anger), and the technique through escape and coping strategy is the action we resort to in dealing with it. This is what is known in addiction recovery as a slip. And slips are to be expected in any kind of healing process.

Our intention here is to be aware of the situations, people, or places that we feel rejected by, and the stress connected to our past events. In many cases it is our interactions with people, but it can also be a place that has some memory attached to it. Our trigger is the first step to acting out against our pain point.

The Trigger in Action

We do not have to react to every situation or person that triggers us to act out. We do have a choice. When we are switched on against a trigger pattern, we may think that doing something, such as binge eating, as a way of coping with our emotions, is somehow going to make us feel better.

In the short run, we treat our pain by slipping back into our old ways. But in the long run, we continue to reinforce our escape route. The habit to escape and avoid our pain, while it feels like the right thing to do, is what keeps us stuck where we are.

When a trigger is activated for the rejectionist, he or she will start to go through a learned process. On the inside, they start to rationalize and feed into the condition. This could be unleashing verbal self-abuse, focusing on a negative thought pattern, making comparisons, or taking part in self-sabotaging actions that further support inferiority beliefs.

People have their favorite trigger techniques that are activated when those situations arise, because when they are switched on the behavior that they have created as their default mechanism channels into a specific action.

Some people start to rationalize the situation and feel somehow entitled to act out. The trigger action becomes an excuse: "Well, he made me do it," or "I had no other choice." In rationalizing their behavior, they are then giving themselves permission to do something about it. They want to get even, by taking the "I'll show them," attitude.

When our pain point is exposed, the situation that caused this is the trigger, and how we deal with it is to apply an escape tactic, a coping mechanism, or a combination of both.

Someone could trigger our pain point of inferiority and vulnerability, but we are in control of our own emotions at any given moment. We decide how to respond, react, and what actions to take. Do not be deceived into believing that "they made me do it." Once we accept responsibility for own responses, we can turn the situation around by choosing to respond appropriately.

Controlling Your Reactions

Remember this: The problem is not what other people do or say but how we react to the situation. Someone you just met could start talking about their most recent achievement. This may come across to us as bragging or trying to show off. If you are sensitive to rejection because of issues with low self-esteem, this conversation could be perceived as a means to undermine your own accomplishments that are not as significant.

Your emotions turn to jealousy or envy, and these feelings can only destroy a potentially good relationship.

But is that what is really happening? Could it be that the other person is just celebrating an achievement they have been working towards for a long time?

Hypersensitivity puts us on edge. Our feelings of inadequacy become triggered by the situation. For example, when we are low in our self-esteem or hypersensitive to our own rejections, we might feel inferior to someone who has a higher education and more job opportunities than we have. Because we are so tuned into our fears of feeling less-than, every word becomes a put down.

We perceive ourselves as intended victims when in fact, the other person was merely trying to show off instead of attacking. In being able to rationalize this and walk yourself through the moment, you can start to rationalize your thinking right there and then. When you see that it is not about you at all, we become less fearful and gain a better understanding of why we feel the way we do.

If our pain point is jealousy, we tap into our feelings of anger and resentment. We may attack that person with our internal "verbal monster," or begin to backstab by telling others how much we "can't stand that snob" (labeling) as a means to defend ourselves (counterattack). Whatever our attack or defense may be, that is where we will also find our best solution to dealing with it.

By recognizing our defensive/offensive strategies that trigger us to respond, this is where we gain personal power over the situation. We can own up to, and recognize that it is our reaction to the situation that challenges the moment we are in.

You lose control the moment you react to an external situation. But if you stay grounded and focused on the moment you can control your urge to react. When we become reactionary, we are acting out of fear. Your fear creates anger or anxiety.

Everyone has his or her own trigger situations. It could be a certain type of character personality or a familiar situation that connects them to a past event. Recognizing what our triggers are before they happen is the key to preventing us from acting out and falling into the negative cycle of defeat.

Action Steps for Managing Trigger Responses

Make a list of people and events/situations that trigger you to feel inferior by activating your feelings of inadequacy.

People: Is there someone who sets you off? What is it about this person that sets you off? Are they constantly bragging about past accomplishments? Is it a type of personality that you don't get along with?

In any case, certain people will trigger you to react: a romantic relationship, a family member, co-workers, or someone you just met for the first time. Relationships are difficult. It is the most volatile area for rejectionists because of their need to compare and seek assurance that they are okay.

Make a list of the people who set you off. Then, next to each name state a reason why this person bothers you. What is it about this person? By writing it out and identifying it you can better manage the situation when it comes up again.

You will likely react or act out many times again, but, if you can see it happening, this puts you in a position to take positive action towards a healthy outcome as opposed to just reacting and hoping for the best.

Events or social functions: Do you dread social events? Is a certain type of event more challenging? If so, what is it that triggers your fear? What are the reasons? Is it because you fear not being able to measure up? Is your shame point going to be exposed? Do you have to give a speech? Are you afraid of attracting attention?

Action Step 1: Control Your Trigger Response

Make a list of the kind of social functions that set you off. Is it interacting with others? Do you feel the need to compare, or do you find yourself in counterattack situations? By recognizing this you can choose to:

1. Go into the situation with better strategies for dealing with it, or

2. Avoid these types of situations altogether.

Catch your trigger before it happens. Once you have identified your triggers, you will know when to expect them. You will still occasionally get caught off guard, but by making yourself aware of these, when it happens, you will be in a better position to deal with it.

By knowing beforehand what your triggers are, you can create strategies beforehand to stop yourself from acting out or feeling like a nobody. Talk to yourself in a positive way. Talk to others in a positive way. You can change your emotions by responding through choice.

Choose a different response. Using the substitution technique [Chapter 10], you can replace your tactics with new, positive techniques that are not self-defeating. You can choose how to deal with your emotion.

You should not disown or ignore your feelings by downplaying them and acting as if they don't matter. Your feelings are real, even if they are not what you want. But how you respond, how you choose to act, makes the difference. Instead of acting out in a perpetual "I'll show them!" attitude, do something for yourself.

Action Step 2: Do Something for Yourself

- Go the gym and have an amazing workout.

- Buy yourself something nice and spend an afternoon with friends talking through how you feel.

- Call someone and invite him or her to a movie or dinner.

- Set a goal and spend 30 minutes a day working on it.

- Take a trip you have always dreamed about.

- Invest in your education: Enroll in an online course or sign up for evening classes at university.

These are substitution techniques, and they are far better than the usual default tactics of lashing out and getting even.

Chapter Recap

Be aware of the situations, people, or places that we feel rejected by, and the stress connected to our past events. Trigger points are activated by a situation we have difficulty coping with.

When confronted by someone who triggers a bad memory from your past, you might respond out of fear. Your trigger point is a defense mechanism.

By recognizing our defensive/offensive strategies that trigger us to respond, this is where we gain personal power over the situation. We can recognize that it is our reaction to the situation that challenges the moment we are in.

By knowing beforehand what your triggers are, you can create strategies beforehand to stop yourself from acting out.

Here are the steps simplified:

1. Identify who and what your triggers are.

2. Catch your trigger before it happens.

3. Choose a different response.

The next chapter shows you how the pain points you experience connect to your triggers. By understanding the dynamics of this, you will be able to handle any difficult situation when it comes up.

Chapter 9

Confronting Pain Points

*"Strength does not come from physical capacity. It comes
from an indomitable will."*

— **Mahatma Gandhi**

We are going to go deeper and talk about the internal pain points that are triggered when our internal defects are exposed. Before we can react with an escape strategy or coping mechanism, something has to trigger the cycle. That switch is the pain point. A pain point is what we experience when our sensitivity to rejection is triggered.

To elaborate on this, the trigger is the external situation, event, or person that sets off the cycle. The pain point is like an open wound that has never healed and is attracted to vulnerable situations that demand sympathy or attention. If you are not careful, tuning towards your pain point for instant relief could be setting you up for failure.

Selecting Coping Mechanisms

Your pain point is an emotional state triggered by an event or set of circumstances. For example, we can feel a sudden stab of jealousy if a friend shows up at a party with a date and we do not have one. Or someone we know has more money, more talent, more opportunity, and always seems to land on their feet while we struggle with everything.

When hit with a situation that challenges our self-esteem or social confidence, one or more of our pain points are triggered. When this happens, our default reaction is to choose an action that diminishes the emotional pain. This is when one of our coping mechanisms are chosen. As a note to what is listed below, most people can have multiple coping mechanisms rather than just one.

Here are a few examples of how people cope with painful situations:

- A woman in an emotionally abusive relationship suffers from being rejected by her partner, and so she looks for a way out to be free of the situation.
- A man at work is ostracized by his coworkers, and he may want to find a quiet place of his own to do his work. These people can go weeks or months without talking to anyone.
- A boy is in a family situation where one or both of his parents reject him for not measuring up to their expectations. He becomes distant and retreats to his bedroom to avoid any negative communication or criticism.
- You are being compared to other people at work, and their evaluations are much higher than yours. You are told that you have to work harder to be at the same level as everyone else. Fearing that you might fail, you take care of the problem by quitting.
- During a speech you accidentally stutter or forget what you are going to say, and someone in the crowd laughs, exposing your shame-based fears and breaking all confidence. You quickly wrap-up the speech and leave the venue, vowing to never give a speech again.

Experiencing rejection is an isolating emotion that drives people to retreat, hide, and put up defensive barriers to keep the "ugly" people out. Detaching from a relationship eventually leads to a breakdown of the marriage or partnership. Detaching from people at work leads to poor employee relations. Detaching from family leaves a child feeling abandoned.

Handling these difficult emotions is disempowering when we have limited skills to deal with them. Let's take the example of the child who was rejected by their parents. This is someone who had love withheld as a child and may feel detached or vulnerable in his or her adult years. In a situation that triggers this pain point, they now look for a means to cope through practicing avoidance tactics.

When they have established an escape route (an addiction, counterattack, or detachment) it relieves the pressure of having to deal with their pain point.

Someone who tries to avoid feelings of vulnerability may jump from relationship to relationship and never commit to any one person. If a woman's pain point is anxiety or loneliness she may isolate and make excuses for not going out. Remember that at the core of every pain point the goal is to avoid being rejected or emotionally injured.

By avoiding what hurts, we invite more of it into our lives. By escaping from the pain that we have never dealt with, we keep it and help it to manifest itself. What we are going to do now is identify our core pain points.

We all have at least one primary pain point we deal with throughout life. Depending on the nature of the experience or condition that pain point will be connected to a favored escape strategy to numb or cope with the feelings you want to bury.

Here is a list of the most common pain points. This is the start of the cycle that we are looking at next. See if you experience any of these pain points:

- Jealousy
- Defectiveness
- Inferiority
- Isolation
- Guilt
- Vulnerability
- Shyness
- Exclusion
- Abandonment
- Chronic worry
- Shame
- Helplessness

It is natural to attach ourselves to the strongest pain point, and, when we attach ourselves to it emotionally we develop defensive strategies for dealing with it. For example, a man whose pain point is "vulnerability" may cheat on his wife or girlfriend; if it is jealousy, he may sabotage someone just to get even or criticize or demean someone just to feel better.

We all have a strategy that we implement at an unconscious level. It feels like it is a part of us, and so we may catch ourselves making excuses by saying "That's just me." But it is not us. It is what we do in defense to protect a fearful ego. It is a learned behavior, and they can be changed if we discipline ourselves to recognize these patterns of defeat as they occur.

The Shame-Based Persona

One of the most damaging core pain points is shame. It is at the center of our self-esteem issues, self-confidence, and social well-being. If you feel great shame in certain situations, you may try to impress people, please them, or go along with everyone just to avoid conflict. Feeling worthless and embarrassed may lead to you hating conversations because you do not know what to contribute or say.

Here are some symptoms of a shame-based mindset for someone we will call Sam:

1. *Sam was made to feel guilty because problems that were experienced in the home were somehow his fault.*

2. *He was ignored, neglected, or abandoned by those who were supposed to love him the most.*

3. *He was rarely, if ever, praised for doing good but criticized for what he didn't do.*

4. *He didn't meet high expectations put on him, and he felt like a failure.*

5. *He was compared to other kids, even siblings, and would hear things like, "Now why can't you be more like that?"*

6. *He would hear his parents talk about other kids and how "smart and talented" they were, which meant he had no support or anyone in his corner.*

7. *He only felt normal when he could isolate himself and be alone.*

8. *He has panic attacks when he has to speak in public.*

9.   *He is constantly comparing himself to others and feeling less than with each comparison.*

10. *He needs reassurance from people: his boss, his partner, or his family.*

As an adult, because love was conditional and withheld, or not all of Sam's needs were met while growing up, there remains bitterness and cold anger. He wants what is owed to him and goes through life demanding it from others.

This drive to "get what he is owed" becomes a demand on others who see him as needy, selfish and overly dependent. Feeling ousted and indifferent, he develops a rejectionist mindset.

Sam's greatest fear is that somebody is going to find out who he is. His protective persona will be exposed. People are going to see right through him and the phoniness. His defects will be brought to light and there will be no place to hide. This is at the core of the shame-based mindset and the foundation for living with inferiority feelings.

Deep within us is a desire to be accepted, loved, and nurtured. Even as adults, these feelings never leave. But instead of seeking it from our parents, we now ask the world for it in our relationships and from complete strangers.

When we do not get it or if the other person cannot fulfill our demands or expectations we develop the victim attitude that says, "Oh, they don't care about me," or "Nobody understands me." These are faulty beliefs.

When you become a victim, you develop a helpless mindset built from fragile confidence that diminishes your sense of worth. This can transition into a form of learned helplessness: a condition where a person suffers from a sense of powerlessness, usually occurring from a traumatic event or a persistent failure to succeed.

As children, we were diminished by the successes we never had. They could have been from failing or never being able to measure up to our parents' unrelenting standards. The defects of those you trusted most were thrust on you. We did not know this at the time, but what we were expected to fulfill placed a heavy burden on us. And because of this, the fear and feelings of rejection becomes a part of us.

It lives within us and we are convinced that it is a part of us. When we have a lack of confidence, especially in engaging with others, we revert back to these feelings of inferiority. It is the automatic response.

Right now, let's focus on what you can do. I will leave this chapter with some action steps that you can take. I promise you that any action that moves you toward a stronger, healthier way of thinking and behaving is going to have a significant impact on the quality of your thoughts and emotions.

Over time, you can heal and learn to be whole again. You are already there; you just need some deep work to move closer towards that goal. It is far from perfection that we are striving for but small victories by overcoming our personal obstacles holding us down.

And give it enough time. Do not expect instant results; rather, focus on building your awareness one day at a time. And one day at a time your feelings of inadequacy and inferiority will become greatly diminished.

Action Steps

Revisit your shame-based childhood. The origin of shame stems from your family life. Someone criticized you or demeaned you. The love you wanted was conditional and not real. See yourself as an adult now revisiting this child. What would you say or do to comfort them?

Visualize this and comfort this child. Do this at least once a day for the next two weeks. After that, take a look at how you are feeling. Connect with your feelings by asking yourself: "How do I feel about this situation now?"

If you are still feeling deep bouts of shame, you may want to consider talking to someone. Sometimes, we have to go to a deeper level to get connected. You can do this more effectively by engaging with someone else who is listening objectively.

List your good qualities. By making this list, you can compare it to the list of defects. Put your defects and qualities side by side and ask yourself "Are these defects real?" If you write down the exaggeration, "Nobody likes me," cross it out and write the truth: "There are many who like me, and some don't."

Everyone has defective character traits, but they also have positive traits. Now, next to each defect, write a positive trait. Be as honest with yourself as you can. Spend at least twenty minutes on this.

Join a support group of positive-minded people. Getting involved with people you can share with is a great way to heal the pain of the past. Connect with people through a mastermind group online or in your local community.

You will find nowadays that connecting online with a group of people who share similar interests and goals boosts confidence and makes you feel a part of something. Get connected with others.

Years ago, when I started doing this, it changed my life. I was no longer "alone" but had found people with whom I could share my thoughts, feelings, and fears. Start to make a list of groups you could join. And this could be anything that is related to your hobbies, interests, or, if you want to go deeper, a group or person who specializes in therapy discussion.

Chapter Recap

We all have at least one primary pain point we deal with throughout life. Depending on the nature of the experience or condition that pain point will be connected to a favored escape strategy to numb or cope with the feelings you want to bury.

Shame is a powerful pain point that causes emotional scarring. To cope with this shame, we resort to behaviors that hurt either ourselves or others.

You can heal your shame by taking steps:

- Revisit your shame-based childhood.
- List your best qualities [and reframe those perceived as negative].
- Join a support group of positive-minded people.

Shame takes time to heal. Take positive action in moderation. Reach out to people you trust and talk about your situation. Do not expect instant results. Focus on building your awareness one day at a time. Your feelings of inadequacy and inferiority will become greatly diminished in the months and years to come.

In the next chapter I will get into the escape tactics and coping mechanisms used to cope with feelings of inadequacy, rejection, and deep-seated beliefs of inferiority. You will then learn the key strategies to recover from this.

Chapter 10

Escape Tactics and Coping Mechanisms

"We all learn lessons in life. Some stick, some don't. I have always learned more from rejection and failure than from acceptance and success."

— Henry Rollins

Escape is used as a means to run away from the feelings of worthlessness. An addiction is an escape pattern used to numb and hide feelings of inferiority. As we will see, it disguises the problem, but fails to resolve it.

There are several ways of using avoidance tactics to cope with difficult moments in life. Let's take a look at these escape strategies and coping mechanisms, and the solutions we can implement to replace them.

Default Tactics: How We Learn to Cope

One pattern of dealing with our painful emotions is to flee from the point of origin causing the pain. When confronted with a situation that triggers fear, vulnerability, or those: "I'm less than," feelings, we take a "flight" action that removes us from experiencing the pain of rejection.

These are what we can call default tactics: We immediately revert to a strategy (coping mechanism) whose purpose is to protect the "ego" and the "self" from the pain point that has been triggered. There are many coping strategies that do this, as we can see from the upcoming list I have included. By default, the reaction we take to a stressful situation is a learned pattern. It is created from years of conditioning ourselves to run.

There is not much thought put into the coping mechanism, because once a reward is linked to the behavior, surrendering to a coping strategy becomes the normal route to take. From an observer's perspective this may appear as "out of control" behavior, but to the person bent on escaping it is the only way out.

Only it is not. We have just trained ourselves to believe so. But like any bad habit, we can recover. We can push reset and set ourselves up with different strategies that work. We are trapped only if we choose to be. That is to say, every time we are faced with a situation where we could be rejected, criticized or ostracized, fear kicks in. Driven by an emotion to survive, this leads to the mind seeking some form of relief.

Now, we know logically that the best way through any problem or adversity is to tackle the problem head on. By overcoming adversity we grow stronger. When we flee through addictive coping practices we are not dealing with the situation.

By avoiding rejection, we just stay fearful of more rejection in the future. By escaping from a social situation because we feel inferior, we just stay inferior. Nothing changes. By learning to reset your habits and coping mechanisms, you will learn to react and take action in a healthy way.

Now, think about a pain point that you have: Are you dealing with difficult relationships? Is there a problem at work? Do you struggle to carry on a conversation in a social situation? Is the fear of criticism so painful that you feel helpless? Is there someone in your life that makes you feel inferior or worthless?

When a pain point is triggered, an escape route or coping strategy is chosen. It becomes your method for survival. You come to depend on it more than anything else. This is the start of how people develop addictions and self-defeating behaviors. They start feeding into a habit to avoid or escape from the pain of dealing with a painful reality. This could be through drugs, alcohol, gambling, sex, or even endless hours of television.

While you are escaping from your pain, what seemingly brings you relief now has a heavy price to pay later. By choosing to numb out these feelings you are setting yourself up for failure later on.

Most people have developed at least one primary escape technique in their life, and many more people have multiple coping strategies depending on the situation they need to flee from. One escape strategy functions as the primary method to cope, but may include other methods of escape as well.

Avoidance Tactics and Coping Strategies

There are many ways people cope with their feelings of inadequacy, rejection, and deep-seated beliefs of inferiority. Part of the cycle of dealing with your uncomfortable emotions is to apply a coping strategy that delivers a specific outcome.

This could be an end result meant to numb out your current reality so that you don't have to relive the pain you went through. If the escape strategy is successful (based on your conclusion) then it becomes your primary method of escape. In other words, you personalize your behavior, even if it delivers an outcome that damages your chances of success in other areas of your life.

The final conclusion is that you stay stuck, but you would rather stay there than experience rejection. One of the core coping strategies in this case is excuse-making, when we convince ourselves that "this is where I belong" because nobody else will accept me. Again, the cycle justifies the situation even when you have a strong desire to do something about it.

People have their favorites for handling those tough feelings of social isolation, fear of being rejected, and not measuring up. You may feed into one or more of these behaviors. Later, we will go over the cycle and how you can minimize and disengage these behaviors. But for now, realize that everyone has at least one of the following coping strategies that act as their primary strategy.

Here is a list that makes up the bulk of the escape and avoidance tactics. Do you recognize any of these coping strategies from the list below?

- Isolating

- Counterattacking (defensiveness)

- Addictive behaviors and numbing the pain

- Blaming

- Criticizing others

- Denial

- Failing to take responsibility

- Avoiding meeting new people

- Avoiding responsibility

- Getting angry (tantrums)

- Being passive

- Sabotaging self/others

- Excessive worrying

- Labeling

- Complaining

- Comparisons

- Holding onto resentments

- Thinking negatively about someone

- Being obsessive about something

- Rationalizing

- Feeling the fear and doing nothing about it.

- Focusing on the past

If you see anything here that resembles your coping strategy, make a note of it so that you can come back to it later when we go over some strategies for dealing with this.

Here are five core areas you could be using escape as a means to cope.

1. Addiction

The first choice for many people is to cope through using an addiction of some sort, and, these days, there are enough addictions to fulfill anyone's needs. Your choice of addiction depends on what works best for you, but the usual contenders are: alcohol, drugs, smoking, or sex. Addictions are tough to break, but there is great freedom on the other side if you break through.

Just to make a note, it is beyond the scope of this book to get into addiction recovery. If you are addicted to any substance or process, I suggest you get professional help. Just keep in mind that addictions could have a direct relation to how you try to escape from painful situations.

The addiction masks the problem, and in itself, is not the core problem. It is merely a symptom of the underlying issues that have not been dealt with.

Action Steps

Is there an addiction that serves as your primary coping mechanism? If so, what is it? If this is something you want to stop doing because it is destructive, then seek out professional help if you have to.

Depending on the seriousness of this, it may be worth it just to talk to someone before making any decisions. If addiction is your core coping strategy, taking action toward eliminating it would make a huge difference in your quality of life.

2. Impressing People and Showing Off (Disproving Your Unworthiness)

Rejection mindset has its power in gaining approval from others. We do this by seeking praise or encouragement without giving any back. We want to be recognized to remove the pain of feeling invisible. We all want to be accepted in some way.

Impressing other people has its origins in childhood. It could be that as a child or young adult, our achievements, no matter how small, were rarely recognized. We were ignored. Our efforts were not validated unless we did something that was extraordinary such as making the dean's list at school or excelling at sports.

This can be a big one for many people, and if impressing others is one of our strategies, observing and replacing this faulty technique is a huge step.

Some ways that we might try to impress people are:

1. Telling everyone about your achievements before they even ask. This usually comes across as a desperate call for attention.

2. Making your achievements or efforts seem superior to another person's. This could also involve sabotaging another person's work or efforts to gain notoriety over your own. It is extreme, but it happens.

3. Seeking approval from others to validate our worth (look what I did, aren't you impressed?).

4. Overemphasizing or exaggerating your success and achievements. Desperate for gaining recognition, we exaggerate what we have accomplished, hoping to impress others. Here is a secret. Most people aren't impressed and don't care.

Action Steps

In what ways do you try to impress people? How could you counteract this? Here is what you can do: Write down and identify the reasons why you feel the need to impress people. What emotions are you going through at the time? Are you feeling inferior to the other person? You want them to like you? You want to be accepted as an equal?

Take time to think on this. For example, you may have an issue with feeling like a failure. Therefore, you try to impress people who are successful. Work through each of the situations when you do this. Map out the conclusions you come to. The next time you are in a situation when the pain point of inferiority or defectiveness is triggered, you can recognize it and stop it before it kicks into action.

3. Going on the Defensive (Counterattacking)

Overly sensitive people tend to get defensive when they feel attacked or criticized. In many cases, what is mistaken as an attack on character could simply be prodding for fun or someone making an innocent joke. But because of our hypersensitivity we fail to see it as any other way.

In other situations, it could be an evaluation at work or being unjustly blamed for something. Whatever the case, the reaction is to take a stand and counterattack. But this can have more damage than good.

People who fight back tend to lash out at times without provocation. They may think that they just had to do it when, in fact, the other person meant no real harm.

Action Steps

Look for ways that you take a counterattack stance. Are you always ready to fight back? Do you look for opportunity to show them who's who and what's what? Do you always feel bad after lashing out?

Watch for those situations when you are ready to attack. This comes when you are expecting something to be done against you, or you are ready to defend your position at all costs, even if you are wrong. Now, what can you do instead of counterattacking?

Here are a few steps to take:

Observe carefully the situations when you are critical of others. Is it when you feel devalued? Unappreciated? Is your shame (pain point) triggered? Do you feel inferior to someone you just met because they are smarter, richer, or more intelligent?

We counterattack as a way to overcompensate. When our feelings of defectiveness are triggered, counter attacking is the coping strategy that is kicked into action.

Make a note of when you counterattack and for what reason. For example, feelings of worthlessness could be a key pain point for you. If it is, when this is triggered, your response is to make up for your worthlessness by choosing a coping strategy such as counter attacking, blaming, or attempting to impress people.

By observing and catching yourself as it is happening, you can choose to end the behavior right away. In most cases we just respond by instinct. But once you see yourself acting out, you can intervene on yourself and put an end to it.

4. Escaping Responsibility

Avoiding situations where you are responsible for other people could be a major area you are sensitive about. This could be a situation at work or at home. A parent could avoid interacting with their spouse or children. At work, you could avoid responsibility or challenges that involve risk. That risk includes the fear of failing at a project or fear of failing to live up to expectations.

When filled with uncertainty and self-doubt, the natural instinct is to flee or hide. By escaping responsibility, we can avoid the stress and anxiety that goes with it.

Action Steps

Are there situations in which you flee from responsibility? For example, taking care of someone, a project at work, or owning up to a mistake. Take notice of the areas of your life that you definitely don't want to be held accountable for.

Then, hold yourself *accountable*. Tell yourself that there is nobody who can do this except you. Push yourself to see the actions through to the end. Do this several times and it will get easier.

5. Self-Sabotage

You struggle to accept yourself as you are. So when you have a little success and things start to go well, you look for ways to derail your success. Self-sabotage is practiced through several methods or tactics.

You could indulge in binge eating, drinking, or overspending to destroy the little good things. If you get a new job that is challenging or there is risk that you could fail, you could sabotage it by showing up late at work or disregarding company policy to get yourself fired.

You want to escape the expectations placed on you to avoid failing before it happens. You do not want any kind of recognition because, deep down, you feel that you don't deserve it.

You commit destructive acts that cause others to ignore you or take you out of the loop. They may say that you are unreliable or cannot be trusted. But just the opposite is true.

Deep down, you want to be recognized, but you cannot allow yourself to be in a position that attracts attention. This is also a way to avoid forming relationships with people. If they get close to you then your cover is blown.

Five Ways You Sabotage Yourself

1. If you are successful in losing weight, you could suddenly go on a binge and gain more weight than you had before.

2. In a new relationship that is going well, you have an affair or start to avoid the person you are dating.

3. At work, you show up late or create conflict in the office to get terminated.

4. If you are showing signs of progress in a recovery program, you could slip back into old behaviors and ruin your recovery.

5. If you are successful at saving some money, you suddenly splurge and spend the money you saved...and then some!

The goal with self-sabotage is to keep you stuck in your "comfort zone." This is related to the cycle we looked at earlier. When you struggle with feelings of unworthiness or the defeatist belief that you are no good, your natural inclination will be to ruin your success through actions that defeat you.

Action Steps

1. Think of a time that you experienced feelings of inferiority or rejection. Now, what is the escape method you used to deal with this? Was this effective? What were the advantages to escaping?

2. Think of an alternative action you could take that would replace your escape tactics. For example, instead of watching TV excessively to relax, you can read for 20-30 minutes or do something creative.

3. In what ways do you justify and give power to your escape strategies? Is it to relieve stress or to help you get through a difficult time? Make a list of the excuses you use that gives power to your escape plan.

Chapter Recap

Escape strategies have only one goal in common: to isolate us from the pain point. A situation that threatens to expose our defects is the perfect opportunity. We all have our own favorite form of escape.

This could be wrapped up in procrastination techniques or self-destructive behaviors such as excessive drug or alcohol abuse. The goal is to avoid pain and escape reality. We pick up these learned techniques from experience and experimentation.

When we find something that works, meaning it relieves our stress or helps to release anxiety, we adopt it as a strategy that works. This becomes our default practice. The more we do it, the more natural it becomes.

Now, let's keep moving on because in the next chapter we are covering *The Breakthrough Cycle* that will give you a big advantage to conquering your rejectionist mindset.

Chapter 11

Guilt-Free Responsibility

"You must take personal responsibility. You cannot change the circumstances, the seasons, or the wind, but you can change yourself. This is something you have charge of."

— Jim Rohn

The reason many people struggle to move forward is that they insist on holding onto their resentments and pain years after the fact. After being criticized, rejected, or mistreated in some way, they want some form of apology from the people who are responsible.

These people who hold onto their grudges are the only ones who can help themselves. They wait for the day when someone else finally gives them the love they deserve which leads to being disappointed all over again.

Meanwhile, their lives grow shorter and their condition does not change; they stay stuck in a rut, blaming and lashing out at others. They are content to blame and point the finger at the people who failed them, and their lives will be filled with resentment, anxiety, and depression.

But you are not like most people. You want it to change, right? Then here is what you have to do:

Stepping It Up

Taking full responsibility for your life and your current emotional state [happy or unhappy] is how we take charge of our lives. By stepping up and putting an end to blaming and finger pointing, you can take control of your own destiny.

You should never put the future of your own happiness in the hands of anyone else other than yourself. When you fully take responsibility for your own emotional well-being you stop putting that responsibility onto other people.

This puts you in a position of empowerment. While spending time with people we like is critical to our well-being, trusting in someone to balance our lives and take care of us could lead to disappointment down the road.

Making a decision to stop blaming others for your unhappiness is taking a healthy approach to being responsible for what happens in your own life. This does not mean you have to forget what happened in the past, but you do have to move on from it. This can only happen when you choose to live life on your terms by making a firm decision and following through with action to create a positive and fulfilling future.

When you wait for someone else to step up and take charge, you lose the chance to make the situation better. You miss out on the opportunity to heal yourself. You give up the moment to take yourself to the next level. Do not wait for someone else to take responsibility for your life.

Here are five ways you can start to practice intentional responsibility in your life:

1. Choose to Act Responsibly

The one factor that makes all the difference is your willingness and courage to accept yourself as you are, defects and all, so you can move on with your life. The moment you decide to take responsibility, that's when a major shift takes place.

But what do I mean by taking responsibility? You are already responsible for many things: your family, getting to work on time, or community events. In fact, people who have an inferiority complex excel at being responsible because they want to please people more than the average person. But that is not the kind of responsibility I am talking about. You need to be responsible to yourself. You owe it to yourself, because nobody else is going to give it to you.

As bestselling author and motivational speaker Brian Tracy said: *"Real responsibility is realizing that nobody is coming to the rescue."*

This means that you have to stop waiting around for someone else to fix your problems. If this is a problem for you, keep this in mind: Expecting others to carry you is another form of self-defeat.

You will not learn to heal when you place unreasonable demands on people. And by unreasonable demands, I mean expecting others to carry your burden, your troubles, and your grievances. Nobody can lift that much and you don't have a right to ask anyone to do so.

2. Own Your Behavior

By taking full responsibility and owning your behavior you gain tremendous power over your emotional state. When you say things like, "I wish he wouldn't make me feel that way," or "She should treat me better than that," you are passing that responsibility onto the other person. You lose power this way.

Having expectations to be liked or treated well all the time are unrealistic. And nobody can make you feel a certain way regardless of how he or she treats you. You take care of the way you react and that is it.

If you react in a defensives manner and lash out you will lose control of your emotions. You will resort to your old behavior of blaming and criticizing. This leads to taking on the victim role. Then the downward spiral begins again, and you have fallen into the defeatist cycle once more.

Own your behavior by observing how you respond. This is a habit you can implement right now. By getting focused and making yourself aware of how you are feeling, how you want to feel, and how you will react when someone is acting in a manner that is unacceptable, you gain greater control over your emotions. Instead of being at the mercy of someone else's response or emotional turmoil, you get to choose how you are feeling today.

3. "It's Them, Not Me." Disowning Your Behavior

When it comes to being rejected, the fear can only originate from one location: Within you. Rationalizing that it comes from others is a lie.

You create the feeling and the fear of being rejected in relationships, social situations, and within your work environment.

It is true that others may "put you down," but this only works with your permission. Nobody can reject you, or at least they cannot project the emotion onto you. Sure, you may be turned down for a job, ignored in public or social settings, or told to "get lost" by a member of the opposite sex, but how you take it is your choice.

People who fear rejection are reacting from an old pattern that exists. If you set aside the fear and decide that it is not going to control your emotions, the situation will not bother you in the least.

As long as you think the external world has power over you and can manipulate you into reacting in a certain way or feeling a certain way, and depending on how you are treated, emotions are going to be influenced by other situations and people at all times.

You can change this today if you decide to. Choose to take responsibility for your emotional state. When you feel the fear of rejection coming on, or you start to experience the trigger that puts you in that mindset, realize that it is up to you how to react. Will you give in to your feelings of inferiority? Or will you talk back and stand up against those negative emotions? You have a choice in your response to everything.

Tell yourself: "I am responsible for my own state. Nobody else is responsible. Only me."

4. Dealing with Blame and Forgiveness

Holding onto blame is a primary coping mechanism. It makes a victim out of us. We spend a part of our lives wanting an apology. By projecting blame onto the people responsible for injury, we keep the hurt alive. It never heals.

I have found only one solution that works best for this: Practice forgiving the people you blame. Visualize yourself having a conversation with the person. Tell them you now understand that, because they were going through their own pain and did not have the skills to deal with it, they projected it onto you.

It is up to you if you want to hold onto it or let it go. By letting it go and replacing it with a "gentle understanding," you set both yourself and the other person free.

This could be harder for some people than others, especially if it involved mental or physical abuse. That makes a much deeper cut, and they may need a professional to talk with. Do what has to be done, but take action right now. Do not wait. You can start with a visualization technique or having a "mirror" discussion and then follow up with any further counseling if needed.

Forgiveness takes effort, and if you cannot forgive the other person at this stage of your life, then that is okay. You can work on forgiving yourself for carrying the burden all these years. Forgive yourself for all the self-criticism or self-sabotage you have caused.

If others were exposed to your negative behaviors or you made them suffer somehow, you can forgive yourself for this too. Make forgiveness a habit and a way of living. By doing this, you set yourself and others free. By not doing it you remain in a state of victimization. Which would you rather do?

5. Make Responsibility an Active Choice

It takes courage to take control of your life. Too many people are caught up in all the hang-ups and resort to petty actions of blaming, criticisms, and holding onto old beliefs that continue feeding into negative behaviors.

In order to reset your old ways, you have to make responsibility a conscious choice. It rarely happens by default. I have found that the mindfulness habit really works in this situation. When we make ourselves purposefully aware of the objectives we are reaching for, through the mindfulness approach, you can add a boost to your responsibility.

For example, choosing to be inferior to others is a choice. Nobody can make you feel this way. Your choices define you, and if you choose to be rejected then you will be. You develop a rejectionist persona where, when you actually feel like a reject, you create more of it in your daily life. If you turn around and say, "That's it; I've had enough. I will not let this situation or person defeat me!" that is the ultimate choice.

Watch for situations that you are trying to avoid taking responsibility. You can see this happening when you criticize, blame, condemn, or talk negatively about someone or a situation.

Denying your responsibility is pushing it away onto others. This is not to say you have to take the blame for everything that happens, but before seeking blame, seek solutions. People who live in fear of being condemned or judged may resort to finger pointing or worse.

You can turn this around by observing your interactions with people. Even reflecting on past moments that happened just today and yesterday, and seeing where you acted with selfishness or tried to escape, can have a big impact on your positive mindset.

Chapter Recap

Be aware of situations that you are blaming, condemning, criticizing, or passing off responsibility to others.

Your actions are your own. Your thoughts and feelings are your own. Make a conscious effort to be aware of what and how you are thinking, feeling and responding.

Owning responsibility for your actions and reactions is the surest way to preventing resentment. Taking full responsibility for your life and your current emotional state [happy or unhappy] is how we take charge of our lives.

By stepping up and putting an end to blaming and finger pointing, you can take control of your own destiny.

The **5 strategies** discussed are:

1. Choose to Act Responsibly

2. Own Your Behavior

3. "It's Them, Not Me." Disowning Your Behavior

4. Blaming and Practice Forgiveness

5. Make Responsibility an Active Choice

Chapter 12

Break-Free Strategies for Living Rejection Free

"Your self-confidence is directly connected to how much you feel you are making a difference in the world."

— Brian Tracy, author of
Eat That Frog!

In this chapter, I am going to present eight strategies that you can implement to create a foundation for building confidence, empowering your self-esteem, and to provide you with the techniques to help push your growth beyond your current limitations.

I recommended that you start right away by taking action and pushing yourself to break free of the "mental chains" of rejection. This means working to eliminate all excuses for feeling crappy about who you are.

We are focusing on getting rid of the rejected victim and building a new persona, the YOU that is free, confident, and filled with a new form of energy. It is time to RESET the way you have been thinking and feeling. The one way to achieve this is through taking specific, intentional action. If you wanted to gain immediate control of your life, this is where we will start.

Break-Free Strategies

Each exercise presented here is simple enough you can implement into your daily routine. It just takes some organization so that you are ready to tap into your mindfulness and know what to do when the situation calls for it.

Let's dive into the strategies:

Strategy #1: Apply the Substitution Technique for Creating Lasting Change

Throughout this book we have discussed several key strategies for changing behavior, discarding old beliefs, and forming a positive mindset to heal our rejectionistic beliefs.

In order to facilitate rapid changes, we can practice the **substitution technique** to further reinforce these changes.

The substitution technique, or replacement technique as it is sometimes called, can solve many problems for us when it comes to working change into our lives. You can find opportunity everyday to use it and, if applied consistently, will help you to develop your relationships, become a better communicator, as well as do things differently to generate better results.

It acts as a major game changer when it comes to healing bad habits and overcoming root negativity. The challenge is in developing the awareness of when you need to use it.

Let's take an example: If you are in the habit of talking down to yourself, let's turn it around using this replacement technique. Instead of talking negatively to yourself with "I suck at this," you could say, "I am now learning how to do this better."

The idea is to reinforce your thoughts with positivity. In the case of feeling rejected, when confronted with a situation when someone says "No", instead of telling yourself, "Well, I've been shot down again", turn the situation around.

Begin by replacing the negative thoughts you have with empowering thoughts. Substitute your first default belief that you're no good with a belief that empowers you. Do not accept any thought that builds on your doubt and fear. Instead of "I am no good" you say, "I am awesome"; "My life sucks" is substituted with "I am so lucky to have everything that I do." And then, you can validate this by referring to the gratitude list you made earlier.

To recap, use the **substitution technique** for replacing:

- harmful, negative words with positive expressions. You can include affirmations that work amazingly well when it comes to forming a positive mindset.

- worry-based, fearful thinking with positive images that encourage immediate action. This will move you closer toward your objectives.

- destructive bad habits with good habits that leads to positive results while creating a better process for doing things.

Use the Substitution Technique for Actions

When you catch yourself criticizing either yourself or others, you can replace this behavior with the opposite action. Instead of criticizing and judging, speak well of others. Build up their reputation. Stop yourself immediately and change this behavior from condemning and verbal criticism to praising the reputation of others.

Challenge yourself to do this for one week. Make it a conscious habit to convert all negative actions, behavior, and conversation into a stream of positive conviction.

Tell yourself "I am awesome!"

Tell others "You are great! I am so happy to have you in my life!"

This technique is a major game changer. Using this alone can have a major impact on how you live your life. Start using it right now!

Strategy #2: Identify Your Positive Characteristics

If someone asked you to list twenty things about yourself that you dislike, I bet you could do it easily. It is always easier to take the way you are used to, such as beating yourself up emotionally or self-criticizing. Let's put an end to this, shall we?

I want you to make a list of ten things you like about yourself. This can be anything you want, as long as it is a positive trait. Then, you will tell yourself why each is a positive trait.

Here is a list I made up so you can see how easy it is:

- I wake up every morning early to get the kids ready for school. This is a good trait because it shows that I am a good parent.

- I hold the door open for people when they are behind me. This is a positive trait because it shows that I am considerate of others.

- I read for twenty minutes every evening. This is a positive trait because it shows that I am trying to broaden my knowledge.

- I wake up early and do ten minutes of exercise. This is a positive trait because it shows I am serious about my health and fitness.

- I help my children with their homework. This is a positive trait because it shows I am intelligent and have patience.

- I am a good friend to the people who know me. This is a positive trait because it shows loyalty and trustworthiness.

Even if you can only think of one or two things right now, that is enough to get started. You can build up your "like list" over the course of the next few days or weeks.

What matters most at this point is you get something down on paper and make it obvious to yourself that you are not all bad. In fact, the more good stuff you discover about yourself, the harder it will be for you to find any excuse to feel inadequate or rejected.

Strategy #3: Give Away As Much Love As You Can…and Start Doing It Now

I knew a man once who, in the final days of his life, said that he had only one regret: He wished that he had loved people more and had given more of himself to the world. He died believing that he had not fulfilled his life's mission because he held back too much. This man said that he had always feared being rejected, and so to not put himself in that situation, he remained isolated and distant.

When you have a situation where you feel rejected by the people who are supposed to love you the most, there is a natural tendency to hold back on giving anything. Afraid of opening yourself up to vulnerability, you keep to yourself. Emotions are clamped tight and little is shared. You have a desire to reach out and be yourself, and to connect with people around you, but, uncertain of the risk involved, you withdraw and connect with nobody.

Introverts are infamous for this, but you do not have to be an introvert to hold back love. It takes great fear to hold onto love, and even more courage to give it away. You think it is courageous to hold onto your love until you find someone who is worthy of taking it, but the opposite is true.

We have to let go of what we are afraid of. For those of us with social fears, holding on tightly is a coping mechanism. But letting go of that fear is the path to healing what we have been afraid of this entire time. Letting go is the pathway to making it all okay.

Gradually let yourself go by giving and opening up pieces of yourself a bit at a time. This could be a kind gesture, a kind word, or a smile to a stranger. I know these seem like simple actions, but as trivial as they may appear, doing this once a day is going to have a major impact on your self-confidence and have a dramatic shift in the way you feel.

Start offering to help people more. Give away what you have been hiding. You are not taking anything with you, so what are you waiting for? I know the fear involved in this. There is the old pain point of vulnerability and being open to injury. Well, if you wait for the perfect moment, you will lose all the moments.

Your social rejectionist persona will not stand a chance against this. I still struggle with this, but those days and weeks when I stop caring about looking silly are the best days for me. On days when I hold on with fear, allowing nobody to get close, it feels like I am putting a clamp around my heart. Do not do this if you want to recover.

By reaching out, you will attract more friendships and you will attract more business as well. People love to do business with those who are open and honest. Let people know what you are all about, and soon, you will be busier than you ever hoped possible.

Action Step #1

Today you have to reach out to one person and say something that you would normally resist saying. This could be as simple as saying "Hi" or letting someone know that you appreciate them. Expressing gratitude is an action.

Action Step #2

Build on your social relationships this week. Make a goal with yourself to connect with five new people a week. Even if it is just a brief introduction, start to put yourself out there. When I first did this, I realized how terrified I was of the world. I have always been very closed-minded emotionally with people in my day-to-day activities.

When it was suggested that I connect with people just by having some simple communication, I started to get to know people. I was no longer trying to impress them, but they were interested in who I was and what I was doing. When I took an interest in them, most people reciprocated. So start to expand on your relationships.

Here is what you can do:

- Organize a get-together party and invite people you do not know.

- Create an online friendship group and connect with people through Facebook or other social media.

- Get interested in other people and what they are doing, what their dreams and aspirations are, and always offer to help if there is anything they need.

Strategy #4: Accept the Things You Cannot Change

There is a saying in Alcoholics Anonymous: "God, grant me the serenity to accept the things I cannot change, the courage to change the things I can, and the wisdom to know the difference."

One of the reasons people stay stuck is the resistance to accepting the things that happened, the events that can't be changed. At a deeper level, they wish that they had been treated better or that things had been different somehow.

Not accepting what happened freezes the event that never changes. Wishing things had been different and wanting to do something about it, we realize that there is no way out. So, we resort to a coping strategy that consumes our life. In other words, we refuse to accept the things we cannot change.

When we can move beyond it, with the courage to "accept the things we cannot change," we empower ourselves to move forward. The wisdom is in knowing and recognizing what can be changed and what can't. Past events cannot be changed. Yes, we know this, but knowing it and believing it are two different things.

We may have spent a lifetime holding onto what was done, but not accepting it. And it isn't easy to accept the mistakes and failures in our past. Things were done and we were injured. We want an apology or someone to own up to his or her behavior that caused us emotional suffering. Whatever it may be, it is time to take responsibility. The past doesn't owe us anything; we owe it to ourselves to start acting differently today.

Years ago, I had to accept that the emotional pain I was holding onto was real and that only I could change it. Only I could unleash the courage to move on. Nobody was going to fix me or take care of my wounded child. I had two choices: move on or stay where I was. Courage is feeling the fear and doing it anyways.

Take a situation that happened and write out what happened. How do you wish it had turned out? What would you do if you could change it?

Make a short list of action steps to move you forward. Have the courage to take that first step. Recite the prayer above and remember it by heart. When you find yourself going back wishing that something had never happened, remind yourself that it is unchangeable. It always was.

But today, you have the courage to make anything happen. So, ask for the serenity to accept what you can't change. This doesn't mean that you have to accept it, just that you need the serenity to do so, or the willingness.

Then, decide what you can change. Is it your attitude toward the situation? A Destructive habit that's keeping you stuck? Work through this, and you will see that you have all the power and strength you need to get through anything. You are only as weak as you believe yourself to be. Look up to yourself, forgive, and focus on your steps taking you forward and not back.

Strategy #5: The Seven-Day Anti-Criticism Challenge

Criticism is a destructive form of negativity. Delivered in the wrong pitch or manner, it can destroy someone's confidence and leave them emotionally "crippled" for life. If you grew up in a very critical environment, and so you know the damage that this can cause. This is why I want you to try the "**Seven-Day Anti-Criticism Challenge!**"

Make a challenge with yourself that you are not going to criticize or say anything negative about anyone no matter what they do. This does not mean you have to be passive and just accept everything they do; rather, seek another way to express your feelings that is not along the lines of criticism or a sharp comeback.

I have challenged myself to do this, and I encourage you to do the same. Within the first few days, I did not make it past a few hours without making a comment, opinion, or criticizing someone for something. In fact, I actually looked for defects in others and then exposed them.

Years of this conditioning led to the bad habit of complaining and a deep sadness I was living with after realizing how critical I actually was. No wonder I was always so miserable!

To combat this, I set up the anti-complaining strategy. It works like this: You have to make a pact with yourself that you will not say anything that damages another person's reputation. This includes everything from backstabbing to sarcastic remarks aimed at tearing down another person's reputation.

This form of negative attacking is extremely damaging, not to the person you are doing it to but to yourself. It is a form of hidden self-sabotage. It is so habitual that you are not even aware you are doing it.

For me, it was normal. So, I started the challenge. It took about two weeks before I could finally get through a full day without criticizing. It was not easy, but this is good. It showed how powerful the addiction was.

Once I stopped, everything changed — My perspective, my mood, and my desire to be right. It also eliminated my need to counterattack, which was one of my core negative coping strategies.

Action Steps

For the next seven days you are going to make a promise to yourself not to criticize or condemn yourself or others in any way. This will require a great amount of self-discipline. And you will likely fail many times. But that is okay. The goal is to eliminate your need to criticize yourself or others.

One of the most damaging practices that kills confidence is your own critical monster. You are going to kill that monster. You can even give it a name such as Whiner, Grouse, or Grump. Start from first thing in the morning and focus on your thoughts. Watch the people and situations that cause you to lash out or feel negative energy.

Buy a calendar and mark off every day that you went without having a critical thought about yourself or another person. By being critical of others you are, in fact, damaging your own self-esteem. By marking it down on a calendar, you can see the progress you are making. Turn this habit around into a positive one, and, when someone makes you angry or criticizes you, go ahead and think something good about that person.

When I started to do this, I felt totally different after I made it to day three. I had no idea how negative I was, not only toward myself but, toward others as well. It is a life-changing technique that drives your confidence up, and continues driving you forward to make solid improvements toward character by eliminating other defects.

Strategy #6: The "Two-Way Mirror Technique"

This is a great technique for calming anxiety and lowering your nervousness so that you can function and be yourself with others. Spend a few minutes with yourself in front of a mirror. It may feel uncomfortable at first, but after a few times, it will become a habit. Do this for just a few minutes in the morning. To save time, do it while styling your hair, shaving, putting on makeup, or brushing your teeth.

Talk positively to yourself. Do not criticize or condemn anything about yourself. Talk to yourself as if you were talking to a best friend. Be the best friend you have ever had. Give yourself positive advice.

Look yourself in the eye and just give yourself advice as if you would give it to someone you care about. Do this technique ten minutes a day first thing in the morning. It builds your confidence and centers your thoughts.

Here are some things you could say:

An achievement you recently had. Praise yourself and give credit for something you recently did. This does not have to be an over-the-top achievement. Just keep it simple.

Talk about the great day you are going to have. Pump yourself up by talking about all the great things you are going to do today. Will you spend time with friends, family, or your children? Will you do something fun that you have been looking forward to? The purpose of this is to get yourself into a positive frame of mind, and to develop a healthy mindset for the day.

Talk about someone you love and admire. This is a great way to start feeling good about people again. Talk to yourself about the most important people in your life.

Talk about someone you have resentment toward. Just as it is important to talk about the people you love, now talk about someone you have a difficult relationship with. Think of one good thing you can say about this person. Imagine he or she is staring back at you as you are having a conversation. This strategy removes the negative energy that builds up when you have to deal with difficult people.

Strategy #7: List the Evidence That Supports You as Defective

When you feel rejected by people or inferior to them somehow, you look for ways to validate the experience. The "victim" in you needs proof that you are not worthy of love, friendship, or attention. This is easy to do. The proof is everywhere if you want to find it.

What you are going to do here is come up with a case against your rejectionism. Just like in court, you are building a case against your feelings of inferiority. You have spent a lot of years living "one down" from everyone and everything.

Now you have to cast aside those feelings of doubt and believe in yourself to rise up and out of the "emotional mud" that is keeping you down. Your goal is to disprove the lies that are keeping you trapped. Show yourself that you are not guilty of being defective.

Here is what you are going to do:

List the evidence that you are worthless or unlovable. Come up with five to ten situations or scenarios that support your belief that "Yes, I am no good."

For example, when I go to a party or social gathering, everyone ignores me. Now this could be a belief that you have, but it is the reality of what you think. Is it true? Are people ignoring you or are they just so preoccupied with themselves that they do not notice you? What evidence do you have that you are being ignored? If someone does ignore you, so what? Does that still prove you are a social reject, or just that they are in a foul mood or being a jerk?

Similar to the example above, write down a situation or event that makes you feel defective. Is it a relationship? Do you feel jealous about someone? Do you feel self-conscious around others because they are looking down at you or judging you?

Write out the situation. Now start to brainstorm to prove if any of this is real. Try to actually convince yourself that others are better than you. Then, work on disproving it. Ask questions like I did above. Do this for every situation you are challenged with when your inferior trap is triggered. Talk back and get angry. Don't just surrender and give in. This feeds into your inferiority and makes you buy into the lie.

Strategy #8: Practice Using Words of Power

Words have an incredible impact on your emotions and mindset. A negative word spoken in the heat of the moment can ruin someone's day, and a positive expression could make it. Using words that empower not only you but also the people around you is one of the best ways to tap into your confidence. Words can alter a negative mindset if practiced over and over again.

When someone is stuck in a negative frame of mind, it is because they have thoughts that are running in negative modes. I realized that when I started to watch what I was saying, most of my words and expressions were foul words, meant to criticize someone else, and derogatory statements to downplay bad behavior.

In other words, I was creating my own misery again and again. And, no amount of self-help material was going to help unless I learned to curb this habit. So I made up a list of positive words. I went online and found empowering quotes. I learned to speak differently and, when I did, I thought differently too.

These positive words became the new way that I spoke. My inferior mind could not hold up the power of a good word spoken. You cannot have negative and positive thoughts occupy the same space at the same time. When you are feeling positive and focusing on this, everything is positive, and you operate from a place of positive energy.

Action Steps

1. Catch yourself when you use negative or self-criticizing words

2. Call yourself out when you say something negative or derogatory about yourself or someone else. Don't let yourself get away with it. Make a note of it and, more importantly, note how you were feeling at that moment. Was it stress or anger? By identifying the situation or persons involved, this could be your trigger.

Chapter Recap

We covered a list of actionable strategies in this chapter:

1. Apply the Substitution Technique for Creating Change: Replace your negative thinking with thoughts that empower you. Use this technique for replacing your beliefs, habits or worrisome thinking.

2. Identify the Positive Characteristics You Like About Yourself.

3. Give Away as Much Love As You Can…and Start Doing It Now.

4. Accept the Things You Cannot Change.

5. Take the **Seven-Day Anti-Criticism Challenge**: Make a challenge with yourself that you are not going to criticize or complain about anyone or anything for 7 days.

6. Practice the "Two-Way Mirror Technique.

7. Practice Using Words of Power.

8. List the Evidence That Supports You as Defective.

Try to implement these strategies at every opportunity you get. They really work to help you break through barriers, build personal and social confidence and give you more "ammo" to combat negative behavior, beliefs and anxiety.

In the next chapter we are going to talk about building social confidence and forging better relationships with people. If you are shy or consider yourself socially "awkward", I'll show you four strategies you can implement to make more friends and secure good relationships with people.

Chapter 13

Building Social Confidence and Better Relationships

"We are constituted so that simple acts of kindness, such as giving to charity or expressing gratitude, have a positive effect on our long-term moods. The key to the happy life, it seems, is the good life: a life with sustained relationships, challenging work, and connections to community."

— Paul Bloom

Building your social confidence with people is the key to managing your fears, doubts, and feelings of inferiority that may creep up on you in conversation. The issues we have surrounding rejection play a powerful role in the way we interact with and handle ourselves in situations that require us to be confident, real, and vulnerable.

The quality of the relationships you create with people adds happiness and value to both your life and theirs. You do not want to miss out on this. That is why bonding with others should be the main goal we focus on to build social skills, and open up our pathway of communication and understanding.

In this chapter we will cover six social confidence strategies you can put into action to build better relationships and deal with rejection when it comes up. By integrating these principles into your relationships at home, with people you just met, or at work, you will soon be creating relationships that last and add true value to your life.

The Social Interaction Strategies

When we fear being rejected, ostracized, or criticized, we close off from the world. In order to protect ourselves against the truth that others may throw at us, we may choose not to engage and bury our true selves deep to avoid emotional injury.

But here is the truth: These fears we have that isolate us from our social connections are self-created. Nobody is making you more fearful than you are. Nobody is rejecting you but yourself. Self-rejection and that inner critic will be like a voice standing behind you shouting obscenities while you are trying to act normal.

Remember this: when we are too focused on the externals, we suffer to control what we cannot. This is why you have to change your thoughts, emotions, and attitude from the inside.

Social Confidence Strategy #1: Condemn Another; Condemn Yourself—Avoiding Harsh Judgments

Judging others openly or in private is a destructive way to kill the reputation of another person. When you judge another person based on their actions, morals, or values that are different from yours, it places them at the bottom of the social ladder for others to clamber over.

Of course, there are times when we are judged for our actions. But judgment could be turned into something better, such as constructive criticism. Rather than judge and blame, we could provide advice, or recommend a better course of action if someone is in the wrong.

Here is something to keep in mind. The judgment you lay on another will eventually come back on you. People who judge harshly, criticize without thinking the situation through, and condemn others through gossip, or bad rumors are setting themselves up for the same unfair trials.

Unless you are born into perfection, the condemnation you deliver eventually becomes your own. You end up eating what you dish out.

One more point to remember is that although some people may listen to your rants, complaints, and opinions of another person's actions, at the same time they are fearful that they will also be on the end of that stick someday. It may actually separate you from the people you are trying to garner attention from and isolate you in a place all your own without any companions at all.

Judging others, passing blame, labeling, and tearing down another person's reputation through harsh criticisms puts you one step away from receiving the same treatment.

Here is what you can do instead. If someone does cause emotional injury that triggers your defenses to want to "react" and take revenge, think things through first. Here are three suggestions:

Approach the Person Directly

Approach the situation objectively and gather solutions for what they could have done differently. Try to understand what they did and why they did it. In many cases we approach a situation logically, try to decipher why something was done, and then start to judge someone based on the limited facts.

Have you ever addressed an opinion or labeled somebody harshly only to realize that you were wrong? Did you have all the facts? Did you really understand that person's point of view? It happens most of the time. In fact, most people are hardly right in their criticism, even though they try to justify it.

Do Not Limit the Playing Field

If you judge harshly you limit the playing field to the amount of friends and variety of different relationships you can have. You close your circle to only those people that think like you, act like you, and accept you without forming opinions.

When this happens you effectively isolate yourself from anything foreign that poses a threat to your ego. This is not a recommended path to take if your goal is to forge healthy relationships. New relationships mean a greater chance for opportunity while expanding your friendships, both personal and in business.

It's about changes you want to make … in others

You condemn someone based on your limited beliefs and then validate this through coming up with all the excuses as to why it is not acceptable. When you condemn another you are pointing the finger around at yourself.

If you judge someone for the way they speak or the fashion that is worn, could it be because you in some way, would like to be just like them or act in the same manner but you cannot? You actually envy what they can do so as a way to make yourself feel more secure you label them for being different.

When you become more accepting of others, you open up the closed doors of your mind. When you become more accepting of yourself you open up the closed doors of your heart.

Take a look around you at all the differences in people. Walk into a coffee shop, sit down, and observe people as they interact, convey dynamic personalities, and are being who they are meant to be. You do not have to form opinions, likes, or dislikes. Just let the moment happen. Train yourself to accept people as they are. Then turn your emotions inside and look at yourself.

Are you judgmental because of fear? Is there something you want to change within but you are afraid to do so? Do you stick with the flock that you feel comfortable with because they do not judge or condemn you?

Step outside of who you are and be the person that you dream of being. Start to do the actions that person would take. Make it a focused effort to change from within. Then you will see real growth take place.

Social Confidence Strategy #2: Assess the situation from the other Point of View

One of the most critically damaging mistakes we make in our social relationships is failing to understand the emotions and thoughts of another person. People form opinions, have ideas, share their experiences openly, and in daily interactions, do things that seem completely bizarre or out of character.

It is called being human, and when we come to gain an understanding of the actions or words expressed by someone else, even if we are hurt by what they have done, it deepens our sense of empathy.

Empathy is what you need to see the viewpoint of others from their perspective, and not only your own.

Similarly, in relationships with our children, spouses, friends and colleagues we encounter situations when the other person is, from our own perspective, wrong in their choice of actions, opinion or words. However, if we step into their shoes and broaden our angle of perception, we can gain a greater understanding of the situation and avoid making false accusations.

Switching POV Is the Key to Successful Social Connections

Henry Ford, one of the most successful businessmen in history, said: "If there is any one secret of success, it lies in the ability to get the other person's point of view and see things from that person's angle as well as from your own."

Similarly, if you have troubles with your spouse, it may be because you just need to put yourself in your spouse's shoes to understand what they are up to. If you have the ability to change your point of view, you can not only avoid a lot of troubles and hassles but you can also predict the next move, which will be helping you in living a successful life.

POV and Rejection

One of the factors that lead to a rejection is that we are only seeing the outcome from our angle. You start to talk to yourself in negative tones and say things like, "I was rejected because I'm no good," or "They must have seen right through me."

Could it be possible that that person is having a bad day? Could it be that you just are not what they needed at the moment? The rejection, as we learned earlier in this book, is not always about you. It is more about the other person in most cases. It is about emotions and circumstances that are largely beyond your control.

Once you move away from the victim role you can easily view the scene from another angle that gives you a broader scope of what is really happening.

Social Confidence Strategy #3: Treat Others as Equals

One of the biggest mistakes people make when trying to forge better relationships is to automatically think that they are somehow above others based on social status, wealth, or position. The truth is that when stripped of all titles and material possessions, everyone is playing on the same field. Some might be faster than others, and others are smarter; but the bottom line is that we all have our strengths and weaknesses.

Equality and Ego

Ego plays a very important part in this role. The ego wants to be better than anyone else. In fact, it does not need any evidence to prove this. It already believes it, and it wants you to believe it too. The ego puts itself above all else. It only cares about self-preservation and it will climb over anyone to put itself at the top of the chain.

Many people, who are put in positions of power, whether those positions are in politics, business, or family, automatically assume that because they have been handed a big title, it puts them above everyone else. The little people are beneath everything else. The ego is a corrupt entity and grasps at anything to justify its existence. Be aware of this and you can control it. Allow it to dominate you and it will.

When you treat people as equals, even if they have less than you do, remember that it is relevant. Just because they have less does not mean they are less. Just because your position or title is above theirs does not mean you are the captain and commander of wisdom.

In today's world the most effective organizations and families are those who train their people to think for themselves. Most people are accustomed to feeling less than they are. They were perhaps raised that way by their parents to be dependent, and so when something comes up, they want someone else higher up [daddy or the CEO] to fix it.

But in fact, most people I have come across, when given the challenge and treated as an equal and not a subordinate, are able to work it out themselves with just the right amount of support needed from friends or mentors. Let them grow up with the knowing that they are free to be who they want to be and that mommy and daddy will accept them no matter what. They are your equals in every way.

Instead of just pointing the finger and assigning blame or lashing out a punishment, take the time to figure out what is going on and what working together to make the situation better can do. You will discover that, by leveling the playing field, you will have more respect and admiration from those around you.

Social Confidence Strategy #4: Confront the Fear of Vulnerability in Relationships

Perhaps the greatest obstacle that prevents us from forging better relationships is the feeling of vulnerability that comes with connecting with others. We are afraid to trust that we will not get rejected or hurt. We put up fronts, act the part, but if someone tries to get to know the real you, the defenses go up and we retreat back into our holes of comfort and safety.

On a superficial level, most people "act" confident, in control, and are quite sure of themselves. Inside, they have fear and uncertainty, doubt, and a deeply hidden inferiority complex. To be afraid, to have low confidence, and to doubt yourself are all things that we fear, and so we try to cover them up with an inflated ego, boasting, or acting confident.

Look Fear in the Eye

Allowing yourself to be vulnerable can be an uncomfortable experience. You feel exposed and open to attack from criticism. You fear that someone may find out who you really are and expose the truth to the world, shattering the false self-image you worked so hard to build up.

The ego, your false self, is always on guard; it has its defenses up round the clock and will do anything to protect its self-interests. This "defense" appears as a friend in times of need; a protector that keeps you safe. It is, in fact, just the opposite.

In order for us to effectively make healthy and deep connections with others, you must concentrate to remove the fear of being vulnerable. Allow yourself to make mistakes. Let others see that you are willing to risk everything in order to be a better friend, spouse, or business partner.

By facing your fears of exposure and vulnerability, by lowering your defenses, you are not making yourself weaker but just the opposite. You are letting others in; you are giving them a chance to know the real you, and what this does is build a level of deep trust. And TRUST is one of the core foundational pillars for building solid relationships.

Chapter Recap

Focusing on building strong relationships is the foundation of overcoming social fears and rejection. The relationship begins with building trust with yourself. Then, you can have a more positive experience socializing and conversing with other people.

Here are the 4 strategies we looked at:

- Avoiding harsh judgments.
- Assess the situation from the other POV.
- Treat others as equals.
- Confront the Fear of vulnerability in relationships.

A few additional communication tactics I recommend are:

- Remember people's names, and address them by their name several times during the conversation.
- Listen and don't interrupt or try to give your opinion before hearing the entire story.
- Complement someone on a good idea when they share their thoughts with you.

Now, in the last chapter, I'll give you twelve effective habits that are going to change the way you think and feel. These habits are critical in helping you to keep making progress and avoid slipping back into old patterns of defeat.

Chapter 14

Twelve Habits to Reset Your Day

"How different our lives are when we really know what is deeply important to us, and keeping that picture in mind, we manage ourselves each day to be and to do what really matters most."

— **Stephen Covey,** bestselling author of
The 7 Habits of Highly Effective People

We have covered a lot of ground in this book up until now. We have looked at the cycle of rejection, how your rejectionism and an inferiority mindset have controlled your life, and the strategies you can put into action to recover from this.

I have shared with you the step-by-step actions for changing your beliefs. We also discussed the different ways people deal with fearful emotions through escape, and the trigger responses compelling us to act out.

Then, we looked at establishing a new, healthy cycle habit to replace the cycle of rejection and implement better strategies for building self-confidence. Now we know that recovery from rejection is a set of forward actions taken consistently.

By taking action, we can push ourselves further than we ever dreamed possible. By confronting the fears that are holding us back, we are now stronger and more resilient to do something about it.

In this last chapter, we will focus on action driven habits you can develop in order to avoid slipping back into old behaviors, fears, and habits. Even after taking intentional action on the recovery steps I discussed earlier, it can be easy to slip back into our old patterns if we just stay where we are. Once we have made progress in our recovery, we should continue to work harder to keep moving forward.

If you are not taking care of your behaviors a little every day, you will find yourself slipping back into the old behaviors that could end up damaging your self-esteem and confidence.

When you let your emotions go unnoticed and negative feelings twist your thoughts, you can revert back to old habit patterns. I do not want that to happen to you. I want you to continue to grow, and to use this book as a guide to keep you moving forward in a positive direction.

Twelve Habits to Build Better Routines

Here are twelve daily habits that you can put into action right away. You can focus on just one habit at a time, or work on building several habits throughout the week.

Some of these habits may seem like common sense or simple. You don't have to adopt all of them. Pick the ones you think would benefit you the most and stick with it for thirty days. Once you hit the thirty days mark, make it a goal to strive for another thirty days.

According to health psychology researcher Phillipa Lally it takes a *minimum of 66 days* to implement a new habit, and could take as many as 254 days depending on the person and circumstances.

If you skip a day in your new habit development, make sure you pick it up again the next day. If you let it go and continue to put it off, you will get out of the habit and have to start over. If you give up after a few weeks, do not beat yourself up over it.

What is important is that you try new things and keep attempting to direct your habits to work for you in a positive way. Building a new routine is encouraging and starts moving your confidence meter up the scale. Even just one new habit has significant positive attributes.

Habit #1: Twenty-Minute Reading Habit

Reading is a great way to stimulate your mind. Reading personal development material keeps you motivated while leveling up your skills in new techniques and strategies. If you are not working on self-improvement a little bit everyday then you risk falling into the habit of doing the same things again and again and probably getting the same results.

Reading the kind of books that make you better today than you were yesterday increases mindfulness and sharpens your overall mental health. This is a solid investment in personal growth.

If your life feels stagnant and you want to change your routine, start reading the kind of material that drives successful people to succeed at what they do best. Spend twenty minutes a day reading a book on motivation, spirituality, money investment, success principles, overcoming fear, or another topic you have a deep interest in.

Do not just sit still and accept life as it is. You can create it in whatever way you desire, but nobody is going to show you how it is done. You have to get out there and make it happen.

I have read hundreds of personal development books over the years with themes ranging from goal setting, habit development, success strategies, and time management. All of these books have had tremendous influence on my choices in life. I made better decisions, improved clarity and focus, and created a new world of opportunity because I put in the time to read the right books. There is a list of books I recommend below.

Action Step #1

Choose a personal development book that you like. You can pick one from the list I have included here [listed below].

Spend twenty minutes a day reading by blocking off that time. I like to use the **Pomodoro Technique** for time blocking. Do this early in the evening and then, if the book has any action steps such as goal setting or visualization, practice that after reading. Of course, twenty minutes is just a recommended time; you can read it for as long as you want.

Action Step #2

Share the books you read with others. Tell them what you have learned through reading and motivate them to take action. If you can, gift a good book to a friend and support each other on your journey.

Below is a list of twelve books you can start with to begin leveling up your game. Make the time to read and you will start to see positive results in both your mindset and attitude.

My twelve best book recommendations to get you started:

- *The One Thing* by Gary Keller
- *Rejection Proof* by Jia Jiang
- *Awaken the Giant Within* by Tony Robbins
- *A New Earth: Awakening to Your Life's Purpose* by Eckhart Tolle
- *Essentialism: The Disciplined Pursuit of Less* by Greg McKeown
- *The Miracle Morning: The 6 Habits That Will Transform Your Life (Before 8AM)* by Hal Elrod
- *Living Forward: A Proven Plan to Stop Drifting and Get the Life You Want* by Michael Hyatt and Daniel Harkavy
- *The Magic of Thinking Big* by David J. Schwartz
- *The 7 Habits of Highly Effective People: Powerful Lessons in Personal Change* by Stephen R. Covey
- *The Power of Positive Thinking: 10 Traits for Maximum Results* by Dr. Norman Vincent Peale
- *The Success Principles* by Jack Canfield
- *Fail Big* by Scott Allan

How to Speed Up Your Reading

Like most people you may struggle to find the time for most things. Reading is an activity that you cannot afford to pass by so I will give you three simple steps I used to read over forty books last year.

Read first thing in the morning. Wake up, drink a glass of water, and open a book. Bypass your email or even looking at the computer until you have put in thirty minutes of reading time.

If you are reading on a device or using the kindle app on your computer or tablet then refrain from checking email or doing anything else. You might have to get up half an hour early to get your reading time in. It is well worth it. This is a positive investment in your personal development.

Choose material that is in line with your goals. There is no point in reading something you do not like. Choose a topic that is in line with your current objectives. For example, I am starting to declutter my house. The book I am focusing on now is *Getting Things Done* by David Allen.

Take Advantage of Small Pockets of Time. Do you get agitated standing in line? How about waiting for an appointment? I am never bored when I have to wait for someone else. You can carry a Kindle reader with you. Or put the Kindle app on your phone or tablet. You have an instant library available for reading anytime.

Action Plan: Set up thirty minutes for focused reading. This can be in the morning or anytime throughout the day. I struggle with reading at night but it works for many people to read before bed. Set a timer, choose your book, and go.

Habit #2: Twenty-Minute Exercise Routine

When life gets busy exercise is one of those activities that we neglect to do. Over time your muscles start to wither away, you move less, and you place blame on yourself for being lazy. What you really need is a short, intensive exercise routine that does not take up a lot of time.

I highly recommend that you do twenty minutes of exercise each day either at home, in the office, or even when driving. This does not have to involve going to the gym; many people do not have the time [or money] for that anyways. You can do great exercises right at home in a short time without the extra cost or time. This could include stretching, yoga, pushups, or intensity training.

Exercise is a way for you to feel great. Working out just in short bursts gives you an energy boost, and not just physically but mentally as well. You will feel refreshed and more alive.

You will discover that when you are doing something positive for yourself, it is hard to sit around and think about your problems or dwell on past events that just recreate old pains. Exercise puts you in a positive state.

When it comes to battling rejection, getting your body into shape stimulates your mind to form a more positive image of yourself. That self-rejection you struggled with will be stamped out. By not exercising you are leaving yourself prone to weight gain, stress, and increasing your chances of getting sick.

Here is a short, 10-minute exercise routine I do three times a week.

Push Ups [2x sets of 10].

You can just use your "palms flat on the floor" version or, purchase a Push-Up Bar that elevates your body while offering stability and hits your muscles harder. Try two sets of these and build up as you go.

Jump rope: It's free and can be done anywhere. I carry a rope with me for those days I am away for the day. Jumping rope increases your blood circulation and is much better than running with less impact on your joints.

You can try 1 set of 50 and then work your way up. If you can do 4 sets x 100 every morning you are giving yourself a tremendous start to the day.

Side Planks: 1 set x 20. Here is a simple version for performing the side plank.

- Start on your side with both feet together and one forearm directly below your shoulder.
- Contract your core and raise your hips until your body is in a straight line from head to feet.
- Hold the position. Don't let your hips drop for the allotted time for each set. Repeat on the other side.
- Time: You can start slow 10-second sets and work your way up.

Lunges: 1 set x 20. Here is a simple version for performing the lunge exercise:

- Keep your upper body straight, with your shoulders back and chin up. Don't look down. Pick a point directly in front of you to stare at so you don't look down. Always engage your core.
- Step forward with one leg, lowering your hips until both knees are bent at about a 90-degree angle.

- Repeat until your set is complete.

There are many variations of home exercises you can do. Are you are stuck in an office all day? You might be sitting at a desk but you can still take advantage of this.

- Calf Raises [sitting]
- Stretching
- Fist curls
- Chair Brace

Exercising for just twenty minutes a day is a major game changer. Lethargy sets in when we just succumb to our schedule or environment. We use excuses such as: "I just can't get to the gym," or "I don't have time," yet many people spend eight hours a day sitting down in an office. You do have time. You just have to tap into how to best use the time you have.

Action Plan: Schedule twenty minutes a day for exercising. If that is difficult, make it ten minutes.

Habit #3: Practice Meditation

When was the last time you actually just stopped, sat down, and did nothing? In today's world of being constantly active, the idea of doing nothing or just allowing yourself to be bored is a rarity. You are surrounded by more distractions, more entertainment, and more ways to escape from reality than ever before. And yet, being bored and doing nothing is just what you need at times.

Years ago, I learned the importance of having a fifteen-minute break from the world. I would find a quiet spot where nobody could interrupt and disengage from the noise. This meant putting away the distractions and letting myself just be.

Meditating for just short spurts a day is a great habit to make you more relaxed while reducing stress levels. You will build increased concentration and focus. By letting your thoughts go and clearing your mind until you feel totally relaxed you can bring greater balance into your day.

Meditation can be difficult at first if you are not used to it. But you can do it anywhere regardless of how much noise pollution surrounds you.

Meditation is nothing more than training your mind to move into a silent place that already exists. You just have to find it and then, once there, focus on staying in that place for as long as you can.

It is easy to start meditating. Here is a simple process I use that works:

- Situate yourself in a secluded location. This can be a room at home or if you are in the middle of a workday, you might have an empty room or space not being used at the office.
- Turn off devices and anything else that could distract you.
- Sit comfortably, close your eyes, and begin deep breathing.
- Observe your thoughts. You don't have to do anything about them. Just let them go.
- Stay focused on breathing. Absorb the sounds and sensations around you.
- Focus on your awareness of the environment.
- Try meditating twice a day. It has so many positive health benefits for both your mind and body.

Once you become experienced at meditating, you will be able to do it anywhere, even on a crowded train or bus. You can focus on your breathing at any time, and move your mind into that quiet space. And yes, meditation is a great practice for dealing with rejection, too!

Action Step

Make a habit of disengaging for ten to fifteen minutes a day several times a day if possible. Just do nothing for the time you are in the zone. Get comfortable with yourself.

Turn off and tune out all distractions. You will find your mind making mental to-do lists and thinking about what needs to be done the next day. But just maintain focus on your breathing; concentrate on every breath coming in and then being exhaled. Do this for fifteen minutes and follow up with some light stretching.

If you have time you can do this twice a day. Once in the morning after waking up, and then in the evening as you start to wind down for the day. At the end of the day our mind and body start shutting down. You should mentally switch off after nine in the evening.

Put yourself into a quiet state. If you have a family or children, wait until they are asleep and then take time out for yourself instead of just wrapping up the night with TV or mindless games.

This is a great habit that will pay you back ten fold. It increases focus and sharpens your mind. You will feel alert and ready the next day. It improves sleep and increases the quality of your life in many ways.

Habit #4: Practice Journal Writing

Writing is an essential part of the recovery process. It puts your thoughts and feelings out there instead of holding everything in and letting it fester into a nasty mess. As we already looked at throughout this book, writing is one of the means of getting connected with yourself. Now what if you were to develop it into a daily or weekly habit to share your process with others? Blogging is a great way to do this.

You can easily set up a blog by signing up for hosting or using a free hosting site. I recommend signing up with a paid host server. For just a few dollars a month you can get your thoughts out there and share them with like-minded people who are going through the same things as you or have a similar interest as you do.

This could also be a great way to reach out and help someone. If social exclusion has always been a stumbling block for you, there are undoubtedly thousands out there still hiding in the shadows of their shame. You could pass along what you now know and help them to move toward recovery.

Action Steps

Block in 20 minutes every morning as soon as you wake up. Use this time for journaling. You can use a basic notebook available at your local stationary store. If you want to get something fancier, check out gratitude journals or visit your bookstore for writing journals.

If you have the time, block in another 15-20 minutes as you wind down at night. This strategy works great for clearing away any negative thoughts that accumulated during the day.

This will have a positive impact on raising your self-esteem and confidence. By putting your thoughts down on paper, you can see subjectively the thoughts and feelings being processed in your mind.

Finally, I would take note of the ways you experienced rejection during the day. Were there any moments that you experienced rejection? If so, how did you react? What feelings did you experience? Now that you can see how you reacted, what will you do differently next time to turn it from a negative to a positive experience?

Make journaling a habit that you continue with for years to come. It will become your #1 habit for personal therapy.

Habit #5: Spend Five Minutes a Day Talking to Someone (you don't know)

I used to avoid meeting new people because my core pain point was in danger of being judged. I thought that if I started to have a conversation with someone, it would not take long before he or she had me figured out. Or I would usually say something stupid, or say nothing at all, being unable to add to the conversation. So I avoided contact and kept every interaction brief with emotions off the table. This isn't a good strategy for making friends.

But reaching out to people we do not know is a sure-fire way to recover from the fear of rejection. It eliminates your rejection avoidance issues if you have any. What I discovered is that many people feel the same way. They are walking around being afraid to engage with anyone, so they keep to themselves. People want to communicate and share with the world. By being the first to open up and say: "How are you doing today?" you could be adding great value to someone's day.

Now, this habit is hard to implement at first. You may still be feeling like "that's just not me," or "what if they just ignore me or think I'm weird?" I can tell you that when I started to put myself out there and I did not care what people thought, my spontaneity exploded. I was meeting people all the time. And those memories stick. Just start with small steps.

Who do I reach out to?

Talk to someone in your company with whom you have never spoken with before or just in brief encounters. Even if it is just a "Good morning!" that is something. By opening up you start to heal quickly and, the other person feels important as well. If they do not reciprocate or are just feeling unfriendly, then so be it. It is not your problem. Go to someone else.

Action Plan

This week, engage in a conversation with someone you do not know. You do not have to walk up to complete strangers. Do it when you go shopping. Have a conversation with the salesperson or cashier. The reason this is important is that it gets you out of the comfort zone.

If the feelings of inferiority have been with you for most of your life, nothing works better than just putting yourself out there. Just say, "To hell with the fear!" and approach people. You would be amazed how people respond to you when you treat them as if they mattered.

If you need help with social confidence and the courage to talk to people in social situations, you can check out *The Art of Witty Banter* by **Patrick King** for additional support.

Habit #6: Make a List of Goals That Inspire You

Writing out your goals is a great habit to move yourself towards taking positive action. You can create a goal portfolio in just a matter of a few hours. With your goals set, you will achieve things that you have always dreamt of but never seemed possible.

I recommend this simple process for setting your goals:

Write down something you have always wanted to do or achieve. Do you want to take a trip? Write a book? Save more money for retirement? I want you to dream big and start writing down all the things you have ever wanted to do and achieve, especially those things that you have always been ashamed to tell anyone!

For years I wrote books and articles, but because of my shame-based personality I never told anyone! I was publishing books on Amazon and keeping quiet about it. That is crazy, but that is what happens when you struggle with the fear of rejection. Even your greatest achievements go unrecognized because you are afraid that somebody is going to find out about it. Let's change that today.

Whatever it is, write down just one goal for now and then use the following process for taking action towards all of your goals.

Take a look at one of your goals and write down five action steps you could take to get moving on it. Is there a course you have to sign up for? A book you have to read? Someone you have to call? Gather some important info from the Internet? Whatever it is, all that matters is that you do something. TAKE ACTION!

Set a completion date. Deciding on a deadline is a very important action. Without a deadline, you could work on your goal forever. Some goals take years to complete; others can be done in a week or less. Regardless, give a concrete date to finish your goal.

Be accountable to others. Years ago, when I started working on my goals, the one area I always failed at was following through on a deadline. And the reason for this was because I had nobody to hold me accountable.

Once you have set your completion date [writing a book, setting your travel plans] let someone know about it. Hell, let everyone know about it. Join an accountability group or put it out there on your Twitter or Facebook. Let everyone know what you are doing. This will create a sense of urgency, which you will find particularly motivating. You can also make a deal with an accountability partner.

If you cannot achieve your goal by a certain date, you will give them [fill in amount here] dollars. Holding yourself accountable is a great way to getting things done. It is the main reason I was able to finish this book on time!

Action Plan

1. Block off three hours during this week to write down your goals. Be clear on what you want. Do this for the next three days.

2. Block off one hour for the next three days [or thirty minutes if time is tight] to develop your goal portfolio.

3. Make it a habit to review your goals at the end of the week.

4. Decide on the specific mini-tasks you will do to move you closer towards achieving your goals.

Habit #7: Plan Your Daily MITs

I made this a habit several months ago and I have not looked back. What you do is this: Before you go to bed OR first thing in the morning, write down the three most important tasks that you are going to do that day.

How it basically works is that, you write down your three most important tasks for the day. Then choose the first task that is the most important of the three and get to work on it. Are you writing a blog? Exercising? This goes hand in hand with the habits featured here and gets you focused on new and fun activities.

How to set your MITs:

1. Write down your three MITs for this day. Your MITs ideally should be related to your current goals for maximum effectiveness.
2. Do your MITs first thing in the morning. If you cannot do everything in the morning due to time constraints, choose the one that you can do. Then, throughout the day, schedule time for tackling the remaining tasks.

If you cannot finish everything today, move the unfinished tasks to the next day. Then, pick up where you left off the next morning. Keep tackling your list and do what is difficult first.

Action Plan

To do these I created the habit of waking up early. By getting up at an earlier time I was able to focus more intensely on what I needed to get done based on my goals for that day/week. If you are struggling with time, you may have to adjust your schedule by going to bed earlier or cutting out on distractions that are wasting time.

Habit #8: Develop the Learning Habit

Is there a new skill you want to learn? A course that you have been thinking about taking to expand your business? A hobby that you want to excel at? Then if so, the learning habit is the way to get started.

In an age of information where we have access to anything it is hard to know where to begin. It feels like we are learning all the time with the amount of information coming in on a regular basis. This is why I suggest that you create a learning habit by committing to a time of day that you can focus and concentrate on the subject you want to learn. If not, you will likely end up chasing everything.

By committing to learning something new, you are increasing your chances of getting a better job, making more money, or advancing in your personal development. Take all three of these advantages and building a dedicated learning session into your routine becomes a no-brainer.

You can learn anything you want to if you know what it is you want to learn. The key is to decide what it is you want to learn. This is also the challenge as we are being tempted by so many other books, courses and information scrambling for our attention.

Here is a **simple 7-step plan**:

1. Identify the skill you want to learn. Write this down.

2. Decide how you will learn this skill. Is it an online course through **Teachable** or **Shareskill**? Will you go to a school or hire a teacher/mentor/coach? Decide the way you will do your training.

3. Connect with the people who you can learn from. Do you have other people around you interested in the same thing? Building a tribe around your area of interest is critical to learning because they can provide you with support when you need it.

4. Decide when you will learn. I find that having a fixed schedule works best when committing to learning a new skill. Doing it when you feel like it means that you'll slack off when the training gets difficult.

5. Decide how much is enough. Are you looking to master this skill, or do you just need to get to a certain level of proficiency?

6. Decide why this is important. What are you looking to gain?

7. Choose your course of action. What actions can you take right now to start moving towards this? What actions do you need to take consistently to learn this skill? For example, if I am learning guitar, I may have to sign up for lessons and practice regularly twice a week.

Action Plan

Decide the skill you want to master and why. Set up a plan to learn and join up with a group of supporters who can hold you accountable. Learn as much as you can and then when you are satisfied, you can put your new skill to work. Or you might decide to move onto another learning curve.

Habit #9: Focus on Being in the Present Moment

Spiritual teacher **Eckhart Tolle**, the bestselling author of *The Power of Now*, wrote, "If your mind carries a heavy burden of past, you will experience more of the same. The past perpetuates itself through lack of presence. The quality of your consciousness at this moment is what shapes the future."

The emotions you have of feeling powerless, inadequate, and inferior are all connected to the past. This keeps the cycle going. When I read this book years ago, it put everything into a new perspective for me. I would like to share this with you.

When you live in the past, that is, when your emotions and thoughts continually run through a cycle that keeps the past events active, you tap into those pain points again and again. It is like putting your finger in an electrical outlet and knowing that you are going to get zapped. But because it is your nature to do what is familiar, people who live in a shame-based lifestyle revert back to this day after day.

This can all change right now.

I already shared with you a technique that you can use to stop this cycle from repeating itself. Make it a habit to focus on your NOW. This will become one of the most important habits you implement. It was for me, but in order for it to happen you have to stay present, and staying present means observing what is happening right now and not what has happened in the past.

It is amazing the power that the past can have on our lives decades later. People who work on their recovery are often surprised when they suddenly realize how they were feeding into that power day after day for years.

The present has power too. You can focus on that power right now. And to that end, make it a habit to stay present. When you find yourself drifting back into memories of the past that trigger your state of inadequacy, bring yourself back.

Create a trigger symbol that keeps you present. A friend of mine wore a colored band around his wrist. When he looked at it, he remembered to stay present. Set your smartphone to chime every so often as a trigger.

Within a few months, you will find that instead of spending seventy percent of your thoughts lost in negative feelings by reliving experiences that ended long ago, you can now enjoy seventy percent more of your life by staying present. Then all you have to look forward to is what is happening now. It is one of the best ways to energize your life. Stay present. Stay in the NOW.

Habit #10: The Money Saving Habit

Money is important. While it may not be everything, having money is certainly better than not having it or being in debt and owing more than you have. While saving money is challenging, it does not have to be difficult. If you make it a habit, you can start saving today regardless of your current financial situation.

Here are a few suggestions for saving money:

Reduce Your Expenses. We all have bills to pay. But some of these bills are unnecessary and could be costing you hundreds [or thousands] of dollars per year. Make a list of the monthly expenses you pay out and ask yourself if there is anything on the list you could either: reduce in the amount of money spent, or eliminate completely.

For example, I recently canceled my newspaper subscription. It was costing $32.00 a month and nobody was reading it. Take a look at things such as: subscriptions or memberships that you might be paying for but no longer using.

Another expense that was costing hundreds per month was eating out at restaurants. By making your lunch at home and taking it to work, you could save a couple hundred dollars a month.

Shop around before buying. When you need something, it pays to compare. Before buying on impulse, look around at various places before making a purchase. Amazon tends to have the lowest prices but there are times I could find cheaper items at a discount shop. It doesn't always have to be new and shiny. Buying used stuff instead of always going for new can save you thousands in $$$.

Borrow items instead of buying. I do buy quite a few books, mostly on impulse through Amazon or at the local bookstore. But you can borrow most books for free. And, if the library doesn't have it, check because they may be able to order it if they have a budget for buying new books.

Pay yourself first. Set up an automatic withdrawal system so that, for every paycheck, you have 10% taken right away. Check your financial situation first to make sure this won't leave you short if money is tight. If 10% isn't doable, you can start with 5%. Put it this way: even if you only put away $100 a month, that is better than nothing, which is what many people end up saving.

In fact, the majority of people are borrowing cash to make ends meet to keep up with mounting bills and expenses. Once you have this worked out, set it up and let it run automatically. $100 doesn't sound like much money, but if you did it for ten years, you'd have over 10G saved. That's' a great start for a future nest egg.

Decide a set amount of money you will save each week or month [depending on how often you get paid]. Decide why you need this money and what it is for. Then set up a system so that you are making your savings plan automatic. This is a great way to save and is the preferred recommended strategy of **David Bach**, the author of *The Automatic Millionaire.*

Habit #11: Assimilate Positive Affirmations

This habit is great for building positive energy, and if you have been suffering from feelings of inadequacy and inferiority most of your life, there is nothing wrong with having more positivity. In fact, it is the only medicine you need. Affirmations and quotes are a great way to rewire your thoughts.

Years ago, when I started to recover from several self-defeating behaviors, a mentor of mine gave me great advice on how to be more positive. He said "Read three quotes a day: one in the morning, one at lunch, and one after dinner. Then, before bed, read all three again."

Within a few weeks, I was walking around reciting these quotes, and they were powerful words that replaced my negative vocabulary. Throughout this book, I used some of these quotes, but I would like to share with you below a short list of ten quotes you can start with right now.

These quotes are from my personal list of favorites that reframed my thinking and I still read on a daily basis.

1. "If fear is cultivated it will become stronger, if faith is cultivated it will achieve mastery." — **John Paul Jones**
2. "You gain strength, courage, and confidence by every experience in which you really stop to look fear in the face. You are able to say to yourself, 'I lived through this horror. I can take the next thing that comes along.'" — **Eleanor Roosevelt**
3. "When I started counting my blessings, my whole life turned around." — **Willie Nelson**
4. "Always be yourself, express yourself, have faith in yourself, do not go out and look for a successful personality and duplicate it." — **Bruce Lee**
5. "We all learn lessons in life. Some stick, some don't. I have always learned more from rejection and failure than from acceptance and success." — **Henry Rollins**
6. "It takes a little bit of mindfulness and a little bit of attention to others to be a good listener, which helps cultivate emotional nurturing and engagement." — **Deepak Chopra**
7. "Your net worth to the world is usually determined by what remains after your bad habits are subtracted from your good ones." — **Benjamin Franklyn**
8. "Doing what you love is the cornerstone of having abundance in your life." — **Wayne Dyer**
9. "Two roads diverged in a wood and I - I took the one less traveled by, and that has made all the difference." — **Robert Frost**
10. "Life is a gift, and it offers us the privilege, opportunity, and responsibility to give something back by becoming more." — **Tony Robbins**

Action Step

Make it a morning habit of reading a list of your favorite quotes. This is a positive action that will set your thoughts for the day. Write the quotes down in a notebook and keep them close by, or mark them on your PC or tablet.

Recite them during the day when you feel anxiety or experiencing a stressful situation. One suggestion is to add to your list of quotes by one a day. At the end of one year you'll have 365 great quotes of wisdom.

Habit #12: Practice the Gratitude Habit

I use to avoid giving out compliments at all costs unless there was something in it for me. Again, giving a compliment meant leaving myself vulnerable. So I would not do it unless I had to. But compliments are another great way to forge amazing relationships. Who does not like to be complimented on a job well done or to be told they look nice?

Some people might rebuff it because they are not used to it. Like you, maybe they have low esteem and rejectionist issues (remember that you are not alone). So give a compliment once a day for a week. Then start to do it twice a day for a second week.

After that, make a game out of it and keep track of how many compliments you give. There is nothing like strong encouragement to make someone feel good, and it is another strong step toward your self-improvement.

Here are a few compliments you can start with:

• Tell your partner or kids how amazing they are.
• Tell someone what a great job they did on something.
• Tell your partner or spouse how nice he or she looks today.

Compliments are difficult at first because as practicing rejectionists we are always looking for reassurance from someone else. The problem with this is that it feeds into our need for feeling like we have to get permission from others before we can feel good about ourselves. This results in a very self-centered approach, and when you wait around for someone to tell you how great you are it becomes an expectation.

So reverse the action. Give it away, and what you give away you will receive back twice as much. But do not give with the expectation of receiving something in return. Accept it as a gift when and if you do.

Creating New Routines

By building a new routine you change the way you behave. When you change your behavior you shift your mindset, priorities, and the way you think. A new routine takes work, and you will feel some resistance at first. That is why you should only focus on building one small routine at a time.

For example: I wake up early, drink a glass of water, do twenty minutes of quick exercises, drink another glass of water, and then read for twenty minutes. It is a simple routine, but I am doing something for my health (exercise and hydration), personal growth (reading), and peace of mind.

Now you have choices that will define you. Not just any choice, but life empowering choices that only you can make. As you finish reading this book I hope you think about some of those choices you would like to make.

Working on Small Habits

Take a brief look at the habits again and think "small stuff." Focus on the little things you can do to avoid getting overwhelmed. It takes time to implement those strategies as habits.

If you want to make big changes, you can do this by focusing on small steps done with purpose. For example, remember that if you want to help someone, you do not have to help everyone at once. Just focus on doing one good thing for one person. Then repeat this again the next day.

If you want to work on replacing a negative belief, focus on one or two positive affirmations that target that belief. Do this for ten to fourteen days. You will see big results in time. Then move onto the next negative belief.

Refer to the negative beliefs we talked about in chapter two or target a specific belief you have. There is a solution for everything, and by focusing on the little stuff you can avoid getting overwhelmed by thinking that you have to do it all.

But if you focus and work on it a little one day at a time, you will gain your confidence, reduce stress and worry, and feel great about who you are and how far you have come. This is not just motivational fluff but real facts. Do what matters a little bit every day, and make it your priority.

Anthony Robbins said:

> *"We often overestimate what we can achieve in a year and significantly underestimate all we can achieve in a decade."*

Think of your life as a long-term project. You are planning it every day in small increments. Set aside one hour a day for the next 30 days to develop your life plan.

What you can achieve in one hour will amaze you if you stay committed to carving out the life you have always wanted to lead.

Preparing for Your Journey

"The journey was a surreal dream. This world was about knowing the person you'd always wanted to be and setting your foot down to it, remembering the person you'd thought you were as a child and rejoicing in its living, breathing actuality."

— Christopher Hawke

This book, *Rejection Reset*, is a book of action, faith, and perseverance. It was written with a single purpose in mind:

To give you the courage, hope, strength, skills, and personal power to live your life free of rejection.

Now that you have read this book, what do you think? Are you ready to take your life to the next level? Can you break beyond the criticism, gripes, and old mindset of yesterday?

I know you can. Your rejection free journey is just beginning.

You can do anything if you stay focused on what you truly want. When you no longer fear rejection but embrace it as a necessary challenge, you will discover that this journey is a wonderful opportunity to embrace your dreams and rise up to a new level of greatness.

The world is not always a welcoming place, but that is because it is full of fearful people. They are looking for a way out of that fear. They need someone to show them what it is like to confront the fears that are stopping them from taking action and living their dreams.

Now that you have some solid skills to work with and you know that you are the creator of your own success, you can show others how to confront the rejection pushing them back and keeping them scared. By doing it scared, we can train our fear to do anything.

Now, let's wrap it up with **four key lessons** to take home.

(1). **Imagine the reality that is yours.** Just take a moment to get yourself into a relaxed frame of mind. Find a quiet spot and clear your head of all thoughts. Now bring yourself into this present moment.

Ask yourself this question: "What could I do with my life if rejection is no longer keeping me scared? What dreams could I accomplish? What relationships could I create? What actions would I take?"

Imagine what can be yours and you can have it.

Reset your day with a renewed vision and expand on your ideas for creating a better life for yourself. Do things differently than you did the day before. Make friends and deepen your relationships with people who are walking a similar journey. In time you will be rewarded with a renewed sense of confidence and a powerful mindset fashioned out of courage and a willingness to never give up.

(2). **Healing is a journey.** It is a lifelong journey. Give yourself time to absorb the lessons of life. Continue to seek the answers to questions and always be asking more.

Small changes day by day and actions practiced consistently over time, while keeping your mind focused on the moment, will produce results that work. You may not see any changes right away, but if you work on expanding yourself just a little every day, within a few months, check out how you are feeling. You should notice a considerable difference in your confidence and approach toward people.

(3). **Rejection is a point of view.** If someone rejects you for something [your idea is not good enough, you are not their type, or you are not the kind of person "we" are looking for] remember that not everyone can have everything.

People with the best looks and amazing talents are still rejected. But when we get turned down, we turn it into a personal vendetta. We might even contemplate a way to get back at that person. You might start to have a line of negative thinking that says, "I'll show him a thing or two!"

For whatever reasons you got a NO, there are also many people out there who have said YES. Looking back on your life, you've probably had more "YES" than "NO." Have you ever succeeded at getting a job? Making a new friend? Getting someone to go out on a date with you? Then most of your life has been made up of acceptance and only a small percentage is rejection.

The odds are in your favor. If you get a YES, you win. If you get a NO, you still win, because the rejection makes you stronger.

(4). **Continue to reject rejection.** When you are no longer afraid of being rejected, you are deciding to empower your life when rejection happens. Amazing opportunities appears when you change your perspective; that is to say, when you start to see rejection as something that can help you and not just hurt you.

The things that do not defeat you give you thicker skin. Why should rejection be any different? Why let it win?

Throughout this book we looked at many strategies for gaining confidence in social situations, like developing your personal power and becoming less scared of the disastrous outcome you were convinced was real. But now we know: The power of rejection exists inside of you. It is yours to own. This means, you can disown it by choosing to reject it.

Do you want to reset the way you have been living? Do you want to stop being a victim of rejection?

Then do not play by its rules. You can reject rejection and be yourself in social parties, on a date, or at home with your family.

The healing starts as soon as you choose to say NO. You can refuse to listen to the negative voices in your mind telling you, "There, you see, rejected again." You can choose to be more outgoing, more confident, and more proactive. You can choose your thoughts and ideas.

Too often we wait for things to change. We wait too long. So stop waiting and start taking action. What is holding you back right now? Is it the idea or belief that you could get rejected, and that would shatter your universe?

If you are doing nothing to change the way you are living your life, you will attract more of the fear holding you where you are. The ability to face rejection again and again builds mental toughness.

Define Your Success

I encourage you to continue to refer to this book whenever you feel like a rejection has defeated you. Refer to it whenever you need a refresher.

Success is best defined when two people work together to overcome impossible challenges. You are not alone in this. We all need to raise each other up so that we can stand on the shoulders of giants and be the best that we can be.

Ask yourself what success means to you. What do you want to accomplish in your lifetime? Who do you want to help along the way? What are you willing to accept, and what will you reject? Keep asking questions to yourself. You will find the answers in time. Continue being a seeker on the journey towards living a better life.

Remember: *You can reset your life, your day, or this minute. You can start over or you can start from where you have never begun before.*

Just keep pushing forward and never give up. You have got this. Do not look back, unless you plan on going that way.

All the best,

Scott Allan

"Perhaps we shall learn, as we pass through this age, that the 'other self' is more powerful than the physical self we see when we look in the mirror."

— **Napoleon Hill**, author of
Think and Grow Rich

Rejection Free™

HOW TO CHOOSE YOURSELF FIRST AND TAKE
CHARGE OF YOUR LIFE BY CONFIDENTLY ASKING
FOR WHAT YOU WANT

Scott Allan

www.scottallanauthor.com

Living the Rejection Free Journey

"Confront the dark parts of yourself, and work to banish them with illumination and forgiveness. Your willingness to wrestle with your demons will cause your angels to sing."

— **August Wilson,** American Playwright

First of all, I want to do two things: I want to **welcome you** into this book *Rejection Free™* and, say **thank you**. You have just made a positive step in taking charge of your life and I am happy to have you here.

I wrote this book because I know the power that rejection plays in all of our lives. If it is allowed to operate unhinged, rejection can control our choices and influence our decisions. If allowed to go unattended, rejection eventually kills our dreams.

You might live in fear of rejection as I had for many decades. But it doesn't have to be that way. In this book I show you that you can win against your fears, rise up to become anything you want, and do whatever you like without living in fear. Whatever rejection issues you have can and will be overcome. I want you to know that you are not alone on this journey.

Fear of rejection can be a very isolating emotion. In order to protect ourselves, we covet our emotions and stay hidden, like small children underneath the blankets afraid of the dark. We try to "play it safe" and take less risks.

The problem with this is that we give up on life-changing opportunities, ideas, and chances in order to avoid the pain rejection brings. This pain not only causes emotional trauma but also can be, for many of us, just as frightening as facing physical injury or even death.

As rejectees, we become like chameleons in a large jungle: we fear being spotted by the predators, so we become adept at blending in, transforming, and disappearing. Ashamed to show ourselves for who we really are, we reject ourselves by staying out of sight. If they can't find you, they can't judge or condemn.

The jungle is the perfect place to avoid attracting attention. This means less social pressure. We can stay below the radar without being asked to do anything outside of our comfort zone. By staying out of sight, you avoid being judged or criticized. We have adapted to a lifestyle that has become our survival zone.

Many of us have convinced ourselves that life is better this way. By hiding from painful situations where the possibility of being judged, ridiculed, or condemned is present, we can control our environment through avoidance. This is not a way to live but a method of survival.

Let me ask you this: What chances or dreams have you given up to stay hidden away? What do you regret not doing because the fear of being ostracized or turned down was just too much to face?

Being rejected is a very real experience. For those people who have attached a deeper, more personal emotion to rejection, it can be completely terrifying.

Consider these questions:

- *What would you do right now if you removed your fear of rejection? What acceptable risks would you take? What opportunities would you explore?*

- *What would you succeed at and commit to if you could remove your feelings of shame? What ideas would you pursue? What would you create?*

- *How can you see your life transforming by pushing through your personal pain of rejection?*

- *Can you imagine a life in which you could be free of your rejection issues once and for all?*

- *Do you struggle with people pleasing, only to end up more alone and confused?*

- *How often do you challenge your fear of being put on the spot?*

- *Do you turn down opportunities for speaking engagements?*

- *Do you stay in relationships because you are afraid of taking a chance on something or someone new?*

- *Do you refrain from asking for the things you really want for fear of being told NO?*

Rejection is not exclusive to any one person or group of individuals. It is something we all go through. The difference is in how we deal with it.

For years I avoided any situation that put my ego-sensitive self at risk. If I was denied something I wanted, it was a personal attack on my character. When someone criticized me or made a disparaging remark, it was because I deserved it for being a "less-than." By making it personal, I became more fearful. As we will see later in this book, rejection comes in many forms and disguises.

In *Rejection Free*, we will learn the specific strategies for how to:

- Choose yourself first, no matter what people think of you

- Ask for what you want without the fear of hearing *NO*

- Break free of rejection in any situation that calls for you to be brave and confront your fears

- Stop trying to please the wrong people and pay attention to the right ones

- Realize that rejection isn't all about you (and how inspiring this is!)

- Put an end to the trap of predictability and the ways it hurts your chances for success.

- Overcome your self-doubt and become great at asking for what you want the most.

- Supercharge your confidence and take charge of your life.

- Desensitize yourself to rejection, so that you can handle anything that comes your way!

Rejection happens to all of us. Nobody is immune to it. However, every time rejection tries to defeat you, you can use the techniques and strategies in this book to defeat rejection instead. You can learn to free yourself from the feeling of shame and the fear of loss. By taking action in the face of fear, you release yourself from an emotional rollercoaster and learn to live your life with confidence.

Now, just to be clear, this book isn't about how to *avoid* rejection. *Rejection Free* is designed to put you in *charge* of your life by dealing with life's situations when you *are* faced with rejection.

When we have developed the life skills for handling fearful situations, we can move away from retreat and take action. This book will teach you how to take your experience of rejection and turn it into every advantage.

Here are some examples of rejection at work in daily life:

- You ask for a raise or vacation at work and your manager says *NO,* your performance level has been below average.

- You finally get up the courage to ask out that girl you've been watching for the last six months ... and then she walks past you on the street with another guy.

- The new book you just published has four reviews, and three of them are negative.

- The bank says *NO* to your loan application because you don't make enough money.

- The dream job you're banking on getting is awarded to someone younger.

- You ask someone for help and they say *NO.*

- Your spouse that you've been married to for twenty years suddenly files for divorce.

- Your presentation you've worked on for months has people walking out.

Building the Rejection Free Lifestyle

I'm inviting you to join me on a journey: It's a journey to a greater sense of freedom. It's a guided plan to provide you with the techniques and deeper awareness to deal with rejection, instead of trying to escape and avoid it. We can't escape from it, but we *can* free ourselves from falling into self-pity and going through the pain of regret for missed opportunities later on in life.

Over the years I have discovered that taking less risks to avoid rejection is not an escape plan but instead, it can become a path to failing quietly. Less risk equals less of everything. The risks I am talking about are the opportunities that we let slip and ignore for fear of losing what we have.

But, it doesn't have to be this way.

There *is* a solution. It is not as difficult as you may think. The way out for you is so close, you are almost there. But you will have to take action and get your hands dirty.

Your other option is to continue living in fear. If you are reading this book, I assume you want the tools to handle rejection and **be free** of the power it has over you.

Breaking out of your fear-based comfort zone—your protective cocoon—isn't always easy, but it's definitely possible. If it were easy, we would all be doing it. But good things come to those that try and persevere.

People do it every day. Look around you. Find someone that has recently succeeded at something.

We have this opinion that all the successful people out there are somehow better than we are. They have tons of confidence and support and on the outside, it appears that their success is guaranteed.

But, this just isn't true.

People who get to where they want to go do so by pushing through their fear. History is filled with many successful entrepreneurs, authors, actors, and musicians who struggled with rejection for years and multiple times before they made it to where they wanted to be.

Harland David Sanders, better known as Colonel Sanders of Kentucky Fried Chicken, had a hard time selling his chicken at first. His famous secret chicken recipe was rejected 1,009 times before a restaurant finally accepted it.

Charlie Chaplin was initially rejected by Hollywood studio chiefs because they thought his style of comedy and acting was too nonsensical to ever be popular or entertaining.

A newspaper editor fired **Walt Disney** because "he lacked imagination and had no good ideas." After that, Disney started a number of businesses that ended with bankruptcy and failure. Pushing through and moving forward, Disney's "lack of imagination" created a billion-dollar empire that is enjoyed by millions of children and adults every year.

Albert Einstein, who did not speak until he was four and couldn't read until he was seven, was expelled from school and was refused admittance to the Zurich Polytechnic School. Teachers and parents believed he was slow and mentally handicapped. Einstein went on to win the Nobel Prize and his work and theories changed the face of modern physics.

One of the most successful TV talents in history, and one of the richest women in the world, **Oprah Winfrey** was fired from as a television reporter for being "unfit" for TV.

In this book we are going to learn to:

- **Take action** when you are afraid.

- **Take action** to break the specific fear of rejection.

- **Take action** when you are paralyzed and feel helpless to do anything.

- **Desensitize** your fear of rejection by doing what scares you.

You may be thinking, "But what action should I take? You say 'take action' like it is an easy thing to do. I would take action, but I don't know where to take action first."

Let's take this one step at a time. First of all, we start with small steps. You don't have to jump into the ocean and expect to swim to the other side of the Atlantic right away, but you do have to at least get your feet wet.

Take small actions every day toward defeating something that scares you and rejection loses its power. In the end, this is what we want: to reduce the power of your fear-based self; to empower you to build a new mindset that strips away all self-doubt.

This can be done. You can do it.

If you are willing to risk yourself by putting the "real you" out there, you could end up creating a specific situation that changes your life significantly. When you take action and do what scares you the most, you are taking charge of your life and your destiny.

By not risking, you risk more. By hiding, you stay afraid.

When you isolate yourself from your pain, as we often do, it amplifies the pain of being alone and heightens the experience of rejection. There is risk in everything. There is risk in doing *nothing* and risk in doing *something*. There are consequences and rewards to everything. We win and we fail at times. Let's stay focused on winning together and breaking free of the emotional chains keeping you trapped.

The ball is in your court.

It's time to play.

Chapter 1

Debunking the Lies
of Rejection

*"I know that when a door closes, it can feel like all doors are
closing. A rejection letter can feel like everyone will reject us.
But a closed door leads to clarity. It's really an arrow.
Because we cannot go through that door, we will go
somewhere else. That somewhere else is your true life."*

— Tama J. Kieves

Rejection is full of lies we believe about ourselves. One of the first
steps to recovery and creating a rejection-free lifestyle is breaking
away from these lies by becoming totally honest with ourselves.
Aligning our thoughts and ideals with the reality of the situation makes
less resistance for ourselves.

These lies keep us from achieving the happiness and freedom we *could*
have. **The lies are what keep you trapped** and continue the pattern of
living in **rejection hell**. This is a term I coined for when we are so
fearful of rejection because of our insecurities that we walk around
expecting it from everyone.

As long as you are acting, behaving, and thinking differently than the
person you want to be, you keep living out these lies every day.

Lies, Myths and Half-Truths

For the most part I always believed that there was something wrong
with me, that my rejection was an illness that only I had contracted; the

rest of the world was perfect and I was flawed. But when you question this logic you can start to see the lies behind the fractured belief.

We all buy into the lies that perpetuate and support this condition. If you convince yourself that you are not good enough, you'll always be trying to prove yourself to someone. Even after having some big wins under your belt, you'll chalk it up to "I was just lucky."

We are flawed in the sense that we have a hard time accepting ourselves as we are; there is this obsession to want to be more, have more, or prove that we do have worth and value. But it's like trying to fill up a bucket with a hole in the bottom.

Big Lie #1: I have to agree with everyone and value his or her opinion above all else.

When you agree with everyone, you don't agree with anyone. You are looking to make friends and please everyone on both sides of the fence; when people find out that you'll just say whatever they want to hear, nobody is going to value your opinion or pay attention to you. What'll happen is that you'll end up rejected again, only this time through your own doing.

We want to be liked, valued, and to be recognized as having a place in this world. But the base truth is that not everyone is going to like you. They might only want something from you such as a favor, so the buy-in you get from temporary kindness doesn't always last.

When you start thinking long-term and support those people who are your real friends, you can stop pretending to be popular and focus on being yourself." By focusing on delivering value to people, we attract the kind of friends and relationships that matter.

Big Lie #2: Getting rejected is personal and it means there is something wrong with me.

The power of a rejection is only as strong as you decide it should be. Two people can be rejected for the same thing: one person takes it personally and gives up; the other says, "Okay, who's next?" and keeps going. You have to keep going if you want to break free.

It doesn't matter if you ask someone out and they say *NO*. It doesn't matter if you apply for twenty jobs and they all say *NO*. It doesn't matter if you write a book and thirty publishers kick it out the door. That rejection you experience that basically says, "You're no good" either makes you or it breaks you. In the end, how you perceive the experience has everything to do with how you'll respond to it. "Rejection" is your opinion (your own judgment of your experience) and not anyone else's.

If someone doesn't like your character, or the way you look or act, just remind yourself these same people are not perfect either. Have you ever rejected someone? Think back to a time that you did and then figure out why. It is that belief at the heart of all this—that "I am inferior to the rest of the world" belief—that keeps us trapped in a rejected state.

Later in the book we will dive into this more, but one of the greatest lies about rejection that everyone buys into is that it is personal. It is the "I wasn't chosen because there is something wrong with me" syndrome. In most cases, what looks and feels personal actually has to do with the other party and not you at all.

There are times, painfully so, when we get rejected for personal reasons. We are too tall, not educated enough or we just don't have the right personality for the job.

But in many situations, we are rejected for reasons beyond our control that has more to do with the other person. The person rejecting you has his or her own personal reasons that extend beyond us. In fact, as I have experienced and what initially perceived as a personal attack on my character was a decision made by someone else based loosely on emotion.

So, take comfort in knowing that, regardless what painful rejection you have been through, we can't always control or be responsible for the decisions of others.

Big Lie #3: Rejection is a permanent condition that I was born with.

Everyone is at a different stage of the process regarding his or her rejection issues. For many, it lasts through high school and then they outgrow it; on the other hand, some people live with it their whole lives. Until you confront your fear of rejection, you will always be afraid of getting ousted or being told *NO*. For many, fear of rejection exists as a permanent condition if untreated.

If you grew up in a home that was critical, harsh, and controlling, your rejection issues are deep and could stick with you throughout your life, resulting in perfectionistic behavior and thinking that keeps the cycle going. Ongoing criticism damages your self-esteem and undermines your confidence at an early age.

If you went through this, your rejection issues will be unlikely to go away until you take action and do the things that you are now afraid to do. Rejection isn't permanent for anyone; sometimes you get a *YES* and many times you don't. Nobody is exempt. What makes all the difference is your reaction to a rejection moment.

Do you believe that you were born rejected? Or do you see it as something you contracted, like a virus that has no cure? The message I will share with you now and throughout this book is: **People are as rejected as they make up their minds to be.**

You can control the outcome of any situation where rejection is an issue. You have a choice to let it defeat you or empower you.

Big Lie #4: I'm different and weird and that's why I am being rejected.

Everyone is weird in his or her own unique way. When we try too hard to be normal it puts stress and pressure on us to perform. You were taught that there is such a thing as "normal" in this world, but that's a lie. There isn't any norm. This leads to perfectionistic thinking. You are not being rejected for being different.

You are being rejected by yourself because you're trying too hard to be something you are not; you are trying too hard to be "normal," a word used by people who are too afraid to be themselves. The next time you look at something and label it as weird, it could just be that you are sizing it up to fit with your own "normal" version of reality.

Your rejection persona is obsessed with "normalcy." It has its own built-in "normal" radar, so when you start acting or doing anything that is out of the ordinary, it sets off red flags and pulls you back. You might feel embarrassed or humiliated when you do something that is weird. You may not be aware of it, because you have been trying to act normal most of your life.

When you are heavily criticized for being you, over the years you become conditioned to not act strangely—it's not acceptable. "Normal people do this." "Normalcy is this way." It's a lie. There is conformity and as long as you are conforming to someone else's vision of how you should be behaving and acting, you'll throw aside your uniqueness and settle for boring over unique.

Big Lie #5: If only I were better, smarter, and more likeable, or, The Self-Rejection Persona.

You need to differentiate between the projections others put on you and what is actual fact. I know the world we live in appears differently. We see supermodels, rock stars, and actors buying lavish homes and getting hordes of attention. We feel cheated. *Where is my share? Why was I born differently?*

As a friend of mine once said to me, "You can't be like Jeff Bezos. There is only one Jeff Bezos, and the job is taken." He was right. The best we can hope for is to be true to ourselves.

For years I compared myself to other people. Not happy with who I was, I wanted to be anyone else but **me**. I thought I was the problem. But in thinking this way, you reject yourself before anyone else can.

If only I had what he had ...

If only I could be in his position ...

If only I were good enough to ...

Why is this happening to me again?

Why am I always excluded?

There, you see? I got turned down again ...

These expectations we have created are not of our own making. We are trying to fulfill the expectations placed on us in our childhood. Do you remember? The pressure to perform, to be better, and to try harder so you didn't disappoint someone, most likely an older sibling or your parents.

As long as you are trying to fulfill the expectations you think others have, you're still living the same pattern over and over. You are trying to recreate what you failed at in the past. Only now, instead of trying to make someone else happy—which you know is impossible—you have put the pressure on yourself.

Self-expectations are the most damaging, because we don't realize that we are the ones who are setting the bar for ourselves. We have convinced ourselves that it's somebody else that expects this of us.

Big Lie #6: I can't succeed because I keep getting rejected, and rejection is a sign that I should give up and pursue something else.

You have the right to be yourself. By choosing yourself instead of rejecting who you are, the big lies are cast aside. What lies are those? *I am not worthy or I am not capable of being or doing what I feel passion about. I don't deserve to get recognition. I am odd and socially awkward.*

All lies. Sure, maybe they have some truth: Maybe you *are* socially awkward. Maybe you *are* lacking in a certain area of life that needs developing. Maybe you *do* have self-esteem issues. But who doesn't have these flaws?

Growing up, there were people close to us who rejected us for our imperfections, and this has carried over to our adult lives. But now we still believe that rejection exists because we aren't good enough or are somehow inferior.

Remember what Henry Ford said: "Whether you think you can, or you think you can't—you're right."

What you think and believe becomes who you are. You will act on your thoughts and make your beliefs real. By giving up every time you go through a rejection, whether it is personal or in business, you are closing the doors on success

The key is to push through the fear and adapt to the pain. This might sound like "motivational hype" but it is the sure-fire strategy that works. Later on, we will look at the strategy for desensitization and how you can make yourself stronger, better, and more adept at handling anything that comes your way.

It takes time to work through these lies we have about ourselves. But as we move through this book and you have time to reflect on what you are learning, you will start to see a new set of truths emerge.

Our thoughts and beliefs have been corrupted over the years. By rejecting who we are, we have failed to become who we most wanted to be. This is the highest form of self-rejection.

Spend twenty minutes a day in silence. Schedule this time in if you need to. Explore your feelings and thoughts during this time. Question the beliefs you have about yourself. Try to see the lies through the negative emotions you are holding on to.

Committing to a daily habit of self-exploration can open up your awareness and encourage you to transform the lies keeping you trapped.

Chapter 2

Choosing a Life Over a Life of Rejection

"We shouldn't romanticize rejection. There's nothing romantic about rejection. It's horrible."

— **Marlon James**

A mentor of mine once said to me, "If you want to make any serious changes in your life, you need to create a vision of the person you would most like to be. This has to be someone you admire and look up to. Someone you would like to be friends with and model yourself after. Someone who inspires you. Create that persona and then put all your efforts into becoming that person."

And so ...

I created Bob.

What About Bob?

Bob hates his job. He hates his life.

He has been working in the same office for fifteen years and lives a menial existence. He comes into work, punches in, punches out, and then, at the end of the day, he goes home to a small one-bedroom apartment. He watches a lot of television and tries not to think about things.

Bob has lost a lot of hope over the years. At times, he even thinks he doesn't have much to live for. Yet Bob has never tried to find a different job. He's never tried to change things, because he has chosen to accept life on life's terms, and retreats from reality.

Bob has never tried anything else that could make him happier. He never takes any chances or tries to meet new people. Bob lives a menial existence, and the worst part is, he knows it.

Every day is the same thing, day in and day out, even though he hates it. It makes no sense. His wife left him because he was so miserable. He lost many friends when he became cynical and down on life.

You see, Bob is terrified of being rejected. That is why he has never tried to succeed at anything else and avoids taking chances where there are no guarantees. For Bob, staying in a *predictable* situation, however painful, is better than going out there and taking the risk of being shot down. By anyone. By everyone.

Bob was rejected a lot in his earlier years. He never did well at school and rarely tried new things. In sports, Bob was chosen last to be on any team. If he asked women out, they would laugh at him before turning him down. He had low grades at school, and that carried over into almost every aspect of his life.

Over the years, Bob has developed a "rejection complex" in his relationship with the world. So, eventually, one day he decides that he won't be rejected anymore. One day, Bob just decides that he has had enough. He wants to live differently. He wants to be the person he dreamed of when he was a kid: passionate, excited, and ready to take on the world.

So, Bob does something completely irrational, unexpected and totally unplanned for. This turning point comes when a friend of his finally intervenes and says, "You are afraid because you create your own fear. You are unhappy because you choose to be unhappy. You fail because you believe in failure."

So, Bob makes an *actionable* decision: Bob decides one day that he is going to choose himself above everything else regardless of what other people think of him. He decides that instead of running from his fear, he will embrace it and use it as an opportunity to learn. Instead of playing it safe and risking nothing, he will take a chance on anything that challenges him, even if it means looking stupid.

Recognizing how he himself has created his own misery through buying into his "rejection persona," Bob goes out into the world. He is scared at first, but he takes action. He meets new people. He takes charge of his life in ways he never dreamed, instead of having life control him.

If he isn't good at certain sports, he finds a sport he *is* good at and excels in it. If there are certain women that laugh at him or don't think he is good enough, he finds the woman of his dreams and just says "To hell with the rest."

When Bob fails to get into a university because of his low marks in school, he doesn't just settle for a low-paying, minimum-wage job; he teaches himself new skills and creates his own work online, selling courses and doing what he loves.

Now, when Bob faces rejection, he turns it into a positive experience by not buying into the expectations that he once imagined the world had toward him. This way, Bob forges his own future. In time, he makes a new set of friends who support his ventures, and he supports theirs.

Bob has changed. He is finally free.

Unlike Bob, most people who still live in fear of what they can't do are trapped in a cycle of rejection that they live to regret.

But how does Bob do this? He doesn't let the world dictate his worth. He laughs at people when they say he is crazy for trying something they normally won't. He does what others say can't be done. Bob has a mission that he is clear about: *"Do the things you've only dreamed of doing, and when you are done, go do more of that."*

Yes, Bob has fear, but he also has something more: conviction. He knows what he wants. He works hard to get it. Despite the obstacles, he has made a decision to push through and keep pushing. Bob knows many people who have given up and accepted their fate as it is given to them.

Bob isn't like that. Now, he can't just lie down on the tracks and wait for that inevitable train to come along and take care of his misery.

Bob is a person of action now. He does it, even in the face of fear. He takes his rejection on the chin and risks more. He has become immune to it. He asks for the things that he wants, even if they tell him *NO*. He is done trying to please other people, and instead lives to make himself happy.

The more he succeeds at this, the more contagious his happiness becomes; he makes it his mission to share this with others. He isn't just making a difference in his own life—everyone around him who comes into contact with Bob wants a piece of what he has as well.

Bob focuses on his dreams and creates a plan—a strategy for getting there. Some people hate Bob; he doesn't do things the way they are supposed to be done, and he doesn't care much about fulfilling their expectations of him. He doesn't care for the haters of the world anymore; he doesn't listen to their opinions, whether good or bad. Bob is free. He still has fear, but it is a minute amount compared to the old Bob.

Now It's Your Turn...

Before we go any further, take thirty minutes to create your own "rejection-free persona" of the person you would like to be. This doesn't mean you have to change yourself in anyway. What we are doing is asking ourselves a question: "If I could act differently in a way that has a positive impact on my life, what would I do? How would I behave? What would I do differently?"

At this point, you may be asking, "Where do I begin? How do I start this journey to freedom? What is wrong with me, that I am so fearful?"

The situation occurs where we trap ourselves. We pass judgments, formulate opinions, and fulfill expectations that lead to more of the same. When we buy into rejection, it solidifies the lies we formulated ages ago about our personal value and self-worth.

In a sense, we are all like Bob: **scared**. We are afraid of what the world is going to think; we are hesitant to put ourselves out there, because people will see us for the phony persona we have tried so hard to hide.

This is the foundation of self-rejection. We are harder on ourselves than anybody else. Staying hidden and out of sight is no way to live your life. It certainly isn't going to put you on the path to fulfilling your master goal or dream.

It is a continuous path to self-defeat. In our attempt to defuse rejection of ourselves, we just create more of what we fear.

How many times have you made a choice based on the desire to make someone else happy?

This is a failed system that just breeds unhappiness and an unfulfilled life. We do make choices—not for ourselves, but for our parents, lovers, partners, and employers. You might be saying, "As long as they are happy, I am happy." When others are happy, we feel good about that. But you need to take care of your own happiness, too.

Are you ready to make a choice?

Bob represents a level of freedom that is available to everyone. If someone disapproves of something he does because it disrupts their schedule, Bob can live with it just fine. Bob has everything he has ever wanted, and not because he had a great education or was popular. Bob has everything he wants because he knew what he wanted and created a clear plan for how he could get it. Bob set himself free by changing his attitude toward himself.

When you shift the attitude and thinking you have about who you are, you care less about what others are judging you for.

Bob made a decision that he would remove every obstacle between him and what he desired. Bob's plan didn't include working in an office all day for someone else, surrounded by people he disliked doing work he hated. Bob had bigger plans. Some people laughed at him. Some helped him.

The people who were there for Bob are his true friends. When you **choose your own** happiness above pleasing others just to gain approval, you see who your true friends are. Then, you can focus on pleasing the people in your life who care.

This isn't to say that we can just do whatever we want to do without consideration for others; it is about being who you want to be by choice, without the fear of being pushed aside or stepped on. When we experience rejection in all of its forms, in most cases we are rejecting ourselves before anyone else has a chance to.

This is about choosing the person you want to be, and not molding yourself into what others think you should be. All of us can have what we want if we can only muster the courage to break through the fear that holds us back from doing the things that we love.

This is the second realization: **You are what you decide to be at any given moment. You choose your actions, thoughts, and direction in life.**

Be prepared for resistance. This mindset goes against how others perceive you and want you to behave. To break free, you need to release yourself from others' expectations.

As we will see in a later chapter, asking for the things we really want is a powerful technique that can be mastered with practice. By asking, you open up the possibilities of what is available.

When you confront your fears and take action, amazing things start to happen. You will come to realize there is a major difference between living *in* fear and living *with* the fear. When we live in fear of being rejected, we develop an "escape-and-evade" attitude; it is easier to run from it than to face it head on.

The other option is to embrace what you are afraid of and develop a thick skin that can handle any kind of rejection. What we will learn to do is find that balance between conformity and delinquency.

One of the core lessons we are going to cover is that you can **choose yourself** above everything else.

How much are you going to sacrifice before you realize that when you accept any situation as something you have no control over, you give up that control and put yourself in a role of someone who is powerless?

The moment you decide that you have had enough of living in fear of being rejected, the changes in your life will begin. This course is not a cure for rejection; it is a tool for dealing with it. You will always have situations and people who say *NO*. It is just a fact of life, no matter who you are.

What we are concerned with here is how you take the rejection. Will you crawl under a rock and never approach rejection again or will you take the rejection you experience and put it to good use?

Chapter 3

Defeating Your
Rejection Persona

*"No one can make you feel inferior
without your consent."*

— Eleanor Roosevelt

I want you to consider the possibility that the rejection you have been experiencing has been largely a product of your own creation. By labeling ourselves as "rejected" or devaluing our own self-worth because of someone else's decision to NOT accept us, we are giving up our personal power to a large degree. In other words, you are allowing another to determine if you are good enough.

If you get turned down for whatever reason, it is because the timing just wasn't right. The person you asked didn't need your services at the time, or the situation wasn't working in favor of the other party because they have specific requirements that cannot be met by you at this time.

This is an opportunity in disguise. By being rejected, you can walk away with an opportunity to make yourself better for the next time around. Let's get out of the habit of looking at this as a failure or negatively thinking, "You see, I knew I was no good."

Now, imagine this scenario.

You are on your way to a job interview. As you walk into the building and are asked to take a seat, you notice the other applicants in the room. There are ten people, five women and five men. They are all decked out in new suits and are as professional as you've ever seen. Your mind immediately starts to undermine your confidence. You begin comparing yourself to these people and wondering if you should really be here.

Self-doubt begins to play with your mind. You begin to ask yourself questions that doubt your confidence:

"I don't have enough education or experience."

"These people are so much younger, refined and look more determined than me."

"What if I blow it? That will just prove I'm a failure."

"What if they ask me something and I freeze up?"

"What if it is a technical question, 'cause I'm really not good at tech stuff?"

"What was I thinking coming here in the first place?"

This is how the path to self-rejection begins. I know—this could happen to everyone. You get nervous and freeze up. You panic and have your moments of self-doubt. It is natural. For the self-rejection persona, it is a daily pattern of self-defeat. You kill your chances before you are given a chance to prove what you can do.

This is how you stay trapped—not by what the world is doing to you, but by what you are doing to yourself. When you can start to recognize the patterns of defeat and the negative thought process that starts tearing away at your confidence, then you can formulate a better plan to deal with it. When you recognize your role in this, you become the "director" of your choices instead of just an actor on stage.

One of the first steps in setting yourself free is to take responsibility for the rejection that you are creating without anyone else's help.

Scaling Up Responsibility

Every decision that you have made has brought you to this moment in your life. When you take responsibility for your current situation, just as it is, you become empowered by accepting your role in creating the situations you end up resenting. By recognizing that you do have control over your life and not everyone else, you move from a self-imposed victim state ("I have been rejected") to a state of deeper personal power ("Rejected? Me? Not so!").

The message that I am sharing with you in this book is:

> The amount of fear you experience through rejection is in direct proportion to the power you give it. In doing so, you are giving people permission to reject you. This has nothing to do with the other side; it is your own choice. If you believe that your rejection is real, it is. This will repeat itself throughout your life as a destructive cycle.

Two people can go through the same experience and feel completely different. One person accepts what happens as part of their growth and personal development; he or she has chosen himself or herself above the perceived rejection.

If you are not choosing your own life, you are rejecting it. If you reject it, you hand over the reins to those other people and let them make your choices for you. When you give up your right to live as a free individual, this is a form of self-rejection.

If living a life of feeling unworthy and inadequate is a prison, then liberating yourself by choosing who you are and how you want to live is the path to freedom. This is the aim: to choose yourself above all else and reject the limitations imposed by yourself.

You have to make clear-cut choices of which you want to be. If not, someone else will make those choices for you. If you don't make choices about your own life, rest assured someone else would make the choice for you. You can only be free when you exercise your right to be intentional about your actions.

It is a massive step when you can let go of self-judging condemnation. By silencing that inner critic that gets the "rejection" ball rolling, you can win the war instead of fighting your daily battles and exhausting yourself in the process.

If you are not responsible for your own life, then who is? If you cannot choose how you want to feel, and you have no control over your own feelings or emotions, then who does? If your emotions and thoughts are not being created and controlled by you, then who is the creator? By asking these questions, you will get the answers you seek.

It begins with taking responsibility for your life. I know this is a tall order. But playing the "victim" role and expecting someone else to carry you is not a healthy option—especially if your goal is to break the cycle of rejection.

Remember this: **You are not rejected unless you give others permission to do so.**

What I want you to consider is, how much of your rejection is actually you rejecting yourself? How much self-rejection are you going to take from your ego? What thoughts are you tuning into when this is going on? It's like the example I gave you for the job interview. You can be sitting alone in a quiet room with people around you and nobody engaging in conversation and suddenly your mind is having a two-way conversation with your fear.

You can control your thoughts. No one has a mind control device manipulating your thought patterns. So much of our suffering is self-inflicted. Responsibility isn't just a choice, but it is an intentional action. You take control the moment you recognize you have control.

Observe the communication you are having in your own mind. This is the "anonymous committee" that steps up when you are struggling with a situation and tries to give you advice.

When you reject that advice, it gets nasty and dishes out insults:

"You just don't have what it takes ..."

"You got rejected because you have no skills ..."

"If only you weren't so obese ..."

"You see? I knew you'd screw up ..."

"Why don't you quit while you're ahead?"

You've likely heard these voices before. They are your inner critics, the dark side of your past struggling to survive in a world you have never really learned to fit in to. When you reject yourself, you create a "tunnel-vision" mindset where every thought you create follows the direction of the one before it.

One put-down leads to another; each negative jab at your character folds into a more powerful punch. Your pattern of self-rejection escalates.

It is a chronic mental habit that fuels the deep convictions that:

- You aren't worth it.

- You don't matter.

- Your opinions and thoughts are useless.

- Nobody wants to know you.

- You should just give up now.

To free yourself, you have to take charge of the thoughts that are killing your spirit. Our bad thoughts that run amok are operating on autopilot; this means you can switch over and take full control of your flight path. If you question the reasoning behind these automatic and negative thoughts, you'll see that they are linked to your past programming. And that program can be overwritten and replaced by positive self-talk.

> "Two men look out the same prison bars;
>
> One sees mud and the other stars."
>
> — *Dale Carnegie, author of*
> How to Win Friends and Influence People

You can start this today, right now, by refusing to be a victim of rejection, by saying "No more!" to the ideas, beliefs, and thoughts that hold you prisoner and add to your fear. Be responsible and start to work on this now.

Putting a Stop to the Blame Game

We have a habit of blaming ourselves when things aren't right. When one of our parents criticized us, we blamed ourselves for not being good enough. When we were compared to others and told that we didn't measure up, we looked down on who we were.

When we were made to feel unlovable by those closest to us, we believed that there was something wrong with us. The words hurt, and with it, that feeling of being abandoned, unwanted, and isolated.

If only I could be better or try harder.

If only I could do things as well as everyone else.

If only I were different somehow.

Years later, no matter how much we struggle to get past these negative feelings, they still stick. We have to make ourselves aware of what our emotions are trying to tell us. You have to question the feelings you have, especially when those feelings are hurting you.

Consider this question: "How can I choose myself when I have spent so many years rejecting who I am?"

When you get that rejection letter from the job you applied for, are they rejecting you? Or did someone else simply have a better skill set than you? How many other people were rejected for the same job?

When you ask someone out and they say no, are they rejecting you, or are you just not their type? Have you been rejected by every person you have ever approached?

When I analyzed all of the situations where I was afraid of being rejected, I concluded: When I thought it through rationally, I realized that people have preferences. I do not always fit with those preferences. There is no rejection here or anything to suspect. It is just the way it is.

When we are super sensitive about our issues with rejection, it feels as if everyone is out to reject us. In fact, it could be that they just desire something else at that time, and it could be that you don't fit those criteria. What we think is rejection is really a special form of "self-preference."

Chapter 4

Self-Rejection and Those Old Voices

"The effects of rejection can either kill your muse or change your life."

— **Jane Champagne**

We often make choices that lead to mediocre results. Instead of choosing the things we really want, we settle for what is available. We also settle for what we believe we are worth, and for many people with rejection issues, that sense of worth isn't too high.

Instead of deciding what matters most to us, we decide to settle for what matters most to other people. Instead of rocking the boat and taking charge of our life, we drift and take life as it comes. And what we end up with is an outcome decided by someone else's needs instead of our own.

Before a job interview, I would come up with all of the reasons why they would probably refuse my application. I visualized myself failing and fumbling my words. I imagined the interviewer asking a question and my not having the answer. I doubted my skills and ability to clearly articulate my thoughts. I set myself up for falling before the fall.

How many times do you let yourself be rejected by your own hand before anyone else even has a crack at it?

It comes from accepting old beliefs that were recorded in our minds a long time ago. Being told that we were no good, being ignored or not chosen, being told *NO* because we just couldn't cut it or didn't have what it takes. The voices of the past, even though they are in the *distant* past, still have power over us.

You need to reclaim your power by making new choices that matter and that give you the upper hand in the game, instead of playing by their rules. These are the choices that empower your goals to take you from a position of powerlessness ("I'll settle for whatever you give me") to a position of power and choice ("This is what I want and I'll settle for nothing else").

You do this when you choose yourself first—in everything you do.

Rejection has taught us many things. It has taught us that self-doubt is first created from within. Others can doubt you (and they will), but it is *you* that doubts you the most.

Others can lack confidence in your abilities, but if you accept their perceptions as the only truth, you'll lose confidence in yourself. However, if you have already built up your confidence and you look at your life from a position of confidence, nobody can take that away from you.

A mentor of mine, who was an excellent salesman, once told me of these rejection seminars in his line of work that would toughen people up for getting told *NO*. He said that some salespeople couldn't get over the rejection that came with the job. They took it personally when a customer wouldn't buy, as if their sales tactics were faulty.

But the ones who made it would just say, "Okay, who's next?" The seminar would focus on the psychological impact of being rejected by customers. And breaking it down so that the sales people were not taking the *NO* personally. It is just a fact. No matter how good you are, there will always be someone who doesn't need what you are offering.

For every 100 sales refused, they would get 1 yes. People won't necessarily buy something from you because you are a nice person; they make purchases for their own reasons. If they say *NO*, it is most likely because they don't really need what you are offering.

But, nobody gets turned down forever. Eventually somebody will say *YES*, and then it becomes a numbers game. The salespeople who became frustrated and gave up after the first couple of weeks took it too personally, because they identified themselves as the cause for being told *NO*.

Life works in the same way. Some will say *YES* and some will say *NO*. You'll be accepted by some and rejected by many more. The people who free themselves from their habitual negative thinking can handle the judgments and words spoken by their critics. After all, who really has the power to judge and condemn?

Most people I meet think they are always right about their opinions. In almost every case, our judgments are misjudgments. When people judge you, do they really know who you are? Can they see inside your heart and make that observation with exact rectitude? Are they qualified to pass blame or to tear someone's reputation apart?

Hopefully, as we move deeper into this book, you can feel yourself opening up to the possibility that rejection is largely a state of mind. Better yet, when you come to accept that you are the one with your finger on the button of your life's changes, it becomes more about taking the initiative for and by yourself.

You have permission to put your self-worth first instead of believing you need approval for someone else. You have permission to hold yourself in the highest regard, without needing it to be validated by rewards or promotions. You can be yourself, without anyone telling you who you *should* be based on his or her own opinions.

Chapter 5

Redefining Your Personal Value

"After rejection – misery, then thoughts of revenge, and finally, oh well, another try elsewhere."

— Mason Cooley

My mentor asked me once, "If you were to place a value on your self-esteem, how much would it be?"

I didn't understand the question. How can you place a value on self-esteem? Or confidence? I was thinking in terms of dollars and cents and so, in a sarcastic attempt to be funny, I said, "A few dollars, I guess. Do you want to buy it?"

He said yes, took out his wallet and laid five bucks on the table. He wasn't joking either. He then said, "I just bought your self-esteem. Now how does it feel?"

My mentor always had a point to his lunacy, even if it came as "tough love" at times, but the lesson was solid:

- Your self-esteem has a value, just like your confidence.

- The amount of value is up to each of us, and nobody else.

Yet, can you remember a time when you accepted the minimum amount for something you held in high esteem? Maybe it was a yard sale and you'd just sold your favorite childhood toy for just a few bucks, because you really needed the money. You knew it was worth more, but you let it go anyway.

So, let me ask you this: How much are you worth? What is the price you place on your own value? How much is your time worth, or your best idea? These are things that have no price tag. You can choose the value of your importance, but nobody else can.

So why do people make choices that are really limitations in disguise?

We complain about our wages—but didn't you accept the job knowing how much it paid? We complain about having no time, and yet we spend hours a day watching TV. Isn't your time more valuable than watching TV instead of working on a project that has the potential to change your life? We complain about the people who drive us mad, but are we not choosing to have them in our lives?

When you decide to choose yourself, you make clear-cut choices about the course of action you are taking, even if that action is in doing nothing. When you meditate or think deeply about something, you're not moving your body very much, but these actions still add value to your life. When you play video games all day or surf junk sites on the Internet, you are engaging in another type of activity that is deciding what your future will look like.

By choosing your actions today, you are choosing how you will live your life tomorrow. By choosing the kind of person you want to be, you are *designing* your life instead of just letting it happen.

When you choose yourself above the rest, this elevates your confidence, eliminates fear and kicks your rejection issues right out the door. The choices in the *now* are the choices of all your *tomorrow*s combined.

We are so used to referring to the future as if it were something in the far-off distance, when in fact, it's the present moment and nothing more. This is all it ever has been.

You create your future through every choice you make in each present moment, which is the only place you really exist. Choose wisely how you will invest your time, emotional and physical energy. What do you want to learn? What courses can you take that will have a massive impact on your career and contributions? What can you participate in that is going to reduce your fear and make you more capable of taking positive action?

Choose your friends. Choose the people you want to spend time with. Who makes you feel so good that you want to spend all day or week with them? On the other hand, who doesn't make you feel this way? Is there anyone that holds you back or draws you into negative thinking?

We can't always choose the people we are surrounded by (for example, a co-worker that is in the same office as you, or a family member that you have friction with). We *can* choose how we will interact with them, and what role we play in that person's world.

You can choose your salary instead of allowing someone else to dictate how much you will be paid; you can choose the work you *want* to do instead of what you have to do for a paycheck. Did you choose your current job because you really wanted to do it, or are you just stuck there filling a chair? If so, why are you stuck? Did you make a choice to be stuck?

You can choose all these things to make your life better, but by *not* choosing, you are also making another choice: **To accept everything as it is and do nothing to better your situation**.

Choosing yourself first is about making **steadfast choices.** It is the ultimate decision and a powerful choice you can make.

It is also not just a one-time thing. I have to constantly remind myself in any given situation that I am the one who makes the decisions.

Nobody else is going to give you a break. You can't rely on someone else to go easy on you just because you have sensitivity issues.

Remember Bob? He cares, but he only cares about the matters that are worth caring about.

If someone has an issue, it doesn't mean it has anything to do with you. Someone is in a bad mood? It's not your fault. Someone is unhappy with something you did and they blame you? Accept responsibility IF you believe it is warranted, but don't just assume that you're to blame.

People are often out of touch with their own reality and the scope of their emotions. They blame, scold, deny, judge, and move steadfastly toward a place of comfortable acceptance that makes them feel safe.

When you are critiqued or judged, it is natural to take it personally. Someone doesn't like your work, your style, your clothes, your character, and because of this, you think it is all you and that you need to change something to gain their approval.

You hear it all the time: *"If only they would be more like this, I'd be happier."*

If you had to change yourself every time someone offered an opinion or criticized you, you would be changing directions every ten minutes. Hold fast to your course: Stay true to who you want to be and not what you are being conned into believing you *should* be.

The Struggle with Self-Acceptance

Rejection always starts as an inside job. We will reject ourselves in 99% of the situations by deciding to not choose who we are. If you try to please everyone, you'll end up giving someone else all the leverage and the power to reject you further.

To some extent, we are all a little self-conscious of what everyone thinks of us. We place a value on an opinion even if it isn't always accurate. You might agree to something just to avoid a look of disapproval or letting someone down, even if it means agreeing to something you didn't want in the first place.

We try hard to be liked, to be accepted, and to be loved. By acting in a way that people approve of, they'll think more highly of us, we think. They'll invite us into their circle—until they figure out that we have been faking it, and then we get ousted out again.

My greatest fear, when I would meet someone new, was: *"What if this person doesn't like me? What if they discover how weird or awkward or uncomfortable I am around people?"*

Everybody has different tastes, needs, and wants. As hard as it is to accept, not everybody wants what you have to give. At times they will reject your skills ("You just don't have the skills for this job") or they will reject your love ("Sorry, you're not my type; I like short, stocky men"). They either want something else or someone else. It is just a fact of life: we are selective creatures and make choices based on our own needs.

What you perceive as rejection is really someone making choices based on their needs at that time. If you struggle with hypersensitivity, every form of rejection becomes a personal barrier. You think it is you, when in fact, it is really the other person or the situation that is driving their choices at the time.

Because someone convinced you in your childhood days that you were not worthy, those negative emotions and feelings and that hurt are still there. When you were criticized, you tried harder to please someone—a parent, a teacher, or someone close. But the criticism continued.

Someone took your confidence away, and now you want it back. This experience has created a condition of hypersensitivity. When you are in a situation that challenges your self-esteem, you become extra sensitive once that fear is tapped into.

Challenge Your Inner Skeptic

The skeptics and critics will always be around. They have nothing to do but target others who are trying to do something positive with their lives. They only have a say in what constitutes your personal worth if you give them that permission, but you don't have to do that. You can keep it. You can decide. **Set aside and schedule time out during the day** to really reflect on the emotions you are experiencing.

Stay in touch with the emotions, thoughts, and feelings that you are experiencing in any given moment. Tapping into your fear will indicate what needs to be approached and handled. If you are procrastinating or resisting taking action, underneath that fear you are practicing "rejection avoidance." This keeps the problem buried, but not solved.

Take time each day to observe your emotions. How are you feeling? What are you feeling? What do you feel anxious about? What can you do right now to face this situation?

Writing your feelings down is an excellent way to bring them to your conscious awareness. Just try beginning each writing attempt with the words *"I feel ..."* and then write whatever comes to mind at that time. Write until you feel you have expressed everything you are feeling.

By putting yourself out there and challenging your fears of rejection, you are opening the floodgates to *real personal empowerment*.

People with a rejection persona think they must be loved by all or hated by everyone. But the reality is, nobody is either loved or hated by everyone. It's not that cut and dry. You try to find acceptance in everyone and sooner or later you'll break your own value systems just to earn that acceptance.

Action Plan

In its negative mode, self-talk is like having someone stand behind you and drill you on all the things you do wrong. The inner critic is a harsh teacher. What is worse is that we pass these negative thoughts on to our children and share our negativity with those around us.

Listen to your self-talker when you are alone. What are you saying to yourself? Do you use negative and demeaning put-downs? The person who is aware of and can direct their self-talk has the rejection habit licked, and this will have a big impact on their life.

Chapter 6

Breaking Free of the Predictable Path

"No matter what challenges you are faced with, or the opinions people have of you, rejection in and of itself from others is not a valid system to predict your future."

— Anonymous

When you avoid being rejected, you eliminate all possibilities of losing, looking bad, or failing completely. You play it safe. You look for the non-fail, safe methods that are guaranteed to reduce your failure rate. Unfortunately, this path reduces your success rate also. This is the path of *predictability*.

Predictability works one of two ways: you either have a guarantee that it will work out in your favor with a positive outcome, or you avoid the situation completely for fear of failing or losing something valuable.

Relying on predictability as a course of action creates a coping mechanism for passive-aggressively dealing with your deeper, unresolved issues.

The questions to ask yourself are as follows:

"What am I protecting?"

"What am I in fear of losing?"

"What do I risk not gaining if I avoid taking any chances at all?"

But the danger of creating a predictable life is that you favor routine over change; although routine serves us well in many ways, if you use it to avoid changing as a means of escape, you are not moving toward freedom but are building larger walls to fortify your personal prison. You are not really free until you can confront the fear of making real choices.

Do you know what happens when life is built on predictable choices? You avoid the difficulties and struggles that others face, in order to eliminate the chances of failing. While this might eliminate your risk factor, by not taking any form of risk and not doing what your heart really wants you end up feeding into your rejection even more. You make it stronger. It prospers, and you fall deeper into the rabbit hole that you have tried desperately to escape from.

Rejectionism is more than just a condition; it becomes a way of life. This way of life chooses the back-end road. You avoid plateaus that lead to higher levels of growth. When life becomes a narrow highway, you make predictable choices that lead to obvious outcomes.

Here is how you create a life of predictability that keeps you trapped:

- You avoid talking about an issue with your spouse or partner for fear that they will not understand you; so instead you complain about the situation to a friend

- You ask for $5 instead of $500 because you know that there is a much better chance of getting less money

- You ask for a date with someone that is an easy catch because the person you really want is out of your league; meanwhile, you fantasize about what it would be like to be with the person you really like;

- You don't try to change your current bad habits even though they are destructive and unproductive; you end up doing the same things repeatedly because there is safety in what you know, even if it doesn't work very well

- You stay in the same job you hate because they all know you and it's a steady paycheck; taking another job and starting over is risky if it doesn't work out

- You don't make any new friends because you prefer the company of old friends that already know you.

It comes down to **risk**. When you make choices based on the risk factor, what you are doing is setting yourself up for success by getting what you are asking for, but not what you really want.

This is what Steve Jobs meant when he said, "Don't settle."

Predictability is about taking second best. You ask for what you can get and not what you really value. Driven by feelings of shame and low self-esteem, living a predictable lifestyle almost guarantees your success.

Make your own list of how you sustain a predictable lifestyle that is actually keeping you trapped.

Now I am not suggesting being predictable is a *bad* thing, because it isn't. But if it is what you do to stay where you are for fear of moving forward, you are doing yourself a huge disservice. Just think of all the opportunities you are missing out on. The experiences you could be having now if you do what you're scared to do. The people you could connect with and places you could go.

I stayed in the same job for fifteen years because I was terrified of applying for a new position. What if I didn't get the job? What if they questioned my education? What if I didn't have the skills or lacked something they needed?

I stayed stuck in relationships I resented and eventually hated because of my fear. I made excuses.

"Oh, we've been together for a long time. It's too late to find someone else."

I avoided large crowds and groups. I hated social functions. People talk about themselves and their accomplishments—I had none to think of. I took no risks and consequently had nothing to brag about. I didn't want people questioning my background or finding out the truth, that I was just ordinary, with no Master's degree or awards to speak of.

I rarely made new friends. I stayed with the same people. It was more predictable that way, and therefore safer. I am not saying there is anything wrong with having the same friends throughout your life—of course not. But are you trying to meet new people? Do you fear social situations because of what they might say or do?

Our choices become pathways that support our rejectionism through controlling the outcome. There is little risk. Life is boring, but it's safe. We don't have to face the shame or humiliation that comes with being rejected.

What is the solution? How do you break out of this life of predictability in order to start living? How is it going to feel if at the end of your life you look back and see all the chances you gave up because you were afraid?

Breaking Your Predictable Pathways

We choose the people, places, and situations that have the least chance to reject us.

It could be an old relationship or a job you've been in for the past twenty years. You might not favor your current situation, but you'll stick with it to avoid changing. Be honest—change requires courage. It takes discipline to find this courage at times.

Being predictable is all about avoiding change; and avoiding change is strongly associated with avoiding rejection. One of the key reasons that we never get beyond rejected child syndrome is because we spend most of our lives hiding from it.

You can't recover if you are constantly on the run.

So, the question you need to ask yourself is this, *"What do I have to lose?"*

In order to break your predictability, you have to do the things that you would normally not do. These are easy to identify. They are the actions that, inwardly, you have always wanted to try but externally you haven't, because of the negative outcome you've already visualized taking place. In other words, you won't because you're not willing to gamble with your humiliation or shame. Your rejection.

But *you can do this*. What is the worst that can happen?

You can break out of the predictable patterns that keep you stuck.

Breaking Predictability

Here are two steps to breaking predictability and putting yourself out there:

Step 1: Take note of your daily habits.

I did this step for a six-month period where I would record my activities every day. This included not only the tasks I did but also the people I associated with, the places I would frequent, and even the food I ate. I discovered that my routine was the same every day. I even took the same route home every night.

By breaking up your routine, just making small changes here and there, you can begin to put some uniqueness back into your lifestyle. When this happens, it expands your risk scale and you'll be ready to try new things.

Why does this matter? You'll get comfortable with risk-taking, and when I say taking risks, I'm not talking about jumping between buildings, but realistic risks. Like meeting new people. Putting your voice out there. Defeating the fear of being judged or criticized.

Then try new things. Go to a different coffee shop where different people hang out. Get out of your familiar zone and into something new. It's natural to have a routine that we are used to, but is your routine keeping you stuck in one place? I realized it was and I wanted to make a few changes that got me trying new stuff.

Step 2: Put yourself in a situation that gets you rejected.

I had a job interview some time ago. It went well even though I didn't end up getting the position. But I knew I wasn't going to get it anyway. I did it on purpose because I wanted to desensitize my fear of interviews. I have never been good at interviewing, so I put myself into a position where I knew I'd be turned down.

It worked. After several more interviews, I didn't care what they thought. I wasn't good enough for their corporation? There were plenty of other opportunities. I was going to look for them and take advantage of everything I could. The funny thing is, the one company I didn't think would hire me actually made me the offer. I didn't take the job, but I am pretty sure that the reason they offered me the position was because during the interview I was relaxed and confident. Sometimes, just not giving a hoot pays off.

When you do something that you usually wouldn't do, you are stepping out of your predictable comfort zone. Everyone has a comfort zone in which they feel totally safe. It's like a protective cocoon. We need this for stability and to feel safe.

If your comfort zone is designed in such a way that it becomes a prison, consider changing up old habits. This doesn't have to be an all-or-nothing maneuver. Taking one solitary action—even a small step—can create a multitude of waves.

Action Plan

Think back to a time in your life when you took a risk on something and failed. Maybe you tried a new line of work or invested in something that lost you money. You asked someone out and they said *NO*. You asked for money but it was only a fraction of what you really wanted. You passed on a business strategy because you feared it wouldn't work out.

Put yourself in this position again and visualize what you would do differently now, if given another chance. How would you talk to the person you are interested in getting to know? How much money would you ask for, and how would you ask for it? What job would you show up to for an interview, knowing full well that you are the person for it?

In order to break out of your comfort trap, visualize it happening. You have to see yourself doing it. Run the scenario through your mind over and over again. Every time you do, you make the vision stronger.

Visually and mentally see yourself taking the actions that you really want to take. Try this for ten minutes a day. Spend time in the morning visualizing how your day is going to go when you do the things that are outside your comfort zone. You will start to break the predictability trap and move closer to setting yourself free.

Chapter 7

Rejection and Love Dependency

"Remember that the best relationship is one in which your love for each other exceeds your need for each other."

— Dalai Lama

After spending most of our lives feeling unloved, ashamed, or humiliated, many of us have internalized the core belief that nobody can possibly love us. We are convinced that we are destined to be alone, and that being alone is better than being rejected.

But when this happens, your love for others becomes clingy, desperate, and eventually hurtful. Love becomes conditional instead of unconditional. You start to love for survival instead of developing healthy relationships.

This fuels the belief that, because you are unlovable, those that are closest to you will inevitably reject you. This in turn lends itself to love addiction or love desperation: when you are so desperate for people to like you, it repels people away.

You either try too hard to get others to accept you, appearing needy and desperate, or you hold yourself back, terrified to put yourself out there on the chance that your love will be thrown back at you. By putting yourself out there, telling people you care is like walking on a ledge afraid of falling off.

Going through rejection in relationships is a major trap for those with a rejection persona. You never really feel accepted or that your love is valued. Criticism and shame are at the front of every interaction.

Our relationships are based largely on trying to hide this rejection. But the more intimate a relationship becomes, the more impossible it is to put up a fake front. As soon as the other person realizes how desperate you are, or that you are not being totally transparent, the relationship ends.

The cycle then repeats itself in the next one. Vulnerability is not an emotion most of us are willing to put at risk, so we hide who we are from the people we want to love the most. In the end it is a lose-lose situation.

In the relationship where rejection is an issue, love is something that is based on conditions. You are lovable if you are good; you are lovable if you follow the rules and do as you are told. You are lovable if you don't embarrass me at the party.

This reinforces the belief you formed in childhood that if you do as we say, you will be loved. Conditional love is always built on a foundation of conditions or requirements that must be met before you receive the love you so desperately crave. This stems from a critical parent or guardian when you were growing up.

Nothing you did was ever good enough, so you tried harder. When it seemed that absolutely nothing was good enough, you gave up and gave into the feeling of being defective. This is one of the origins of developing a rejection persona.

First of all, conditional love isn't real love. This kind of love falls under the pretense that "I'll love you IF you …"

To become worthy of another person's approval, you have to earn it somehow. It is like going to work and getting paid a salary. We will pay you this much IF you do the job we expect. **Love isn't a condition.** It is an absolute. It has to be, or else it becomes a negotiation.

If you have children, then you know what this means. You love your children without conditions. Yes, they misbehave and act up and do the things you don't want them to do. They might even get into real trouble someday. But they are still your kids. Unconditional.

Now, in your daily life, most people you associate with are not going to love you unconditionally. You will be met with conditions in most situations in your life. People will like you if you do this or that; you do a good job for your manager, you're on her good side; you screw up, you're on her other side.

The rejection persona has become accustomed to this conditioned way of love. However, many people who crave love crave unconditional love. But because you are conditioned, you try to meet all the conditions that everyone places on you in hopes you fulfill another person's wishes and receive that unconditional acceptance you're seeking. It's a vicious cycle.

We spend most of our lives "seeking," searching for the things that are missing on the inside. We missed out on love when we were kids, and now we want someone else to give it to us. Our parents didn't give us the love we should have received, and now there is a big hole in our lives where love should be.

The dilemma is, you'll spend the rest of your life trying to fill that big hole if you are searching for it "out there." The external world cannot give you anything that is lasting or permanent.

You were never accepted or recognized for anything of value, so you feel worthless. The result: you seek acceptance and worth from others. And how much do you need before you can feel totally fulfilled? It's like a bottomless pit, and there is no amount of encouragement or positive reinforcement that anybody can give you that would ever be good enough.

When you spend your life seeking and expecting some form of payback, you want what is owed to you: love, love, and more love. As a child you were devalued and underappreciated. School marks were never good enough, you were poor at sports, or at home you always seemed to be "in the way."

It is painful to accept, but if you do the deep analysis work and come to terms with your rejection persona in relationships, you will reach this conclusion: The love you are trying to find and extract from your relationships will never be enough. It isn't the same thing, not the way your parents could have given it to you. You will only become frustrated and start rejecting your partner or putting them down as a means to defend your position in the relationship. Power struggles will then erupt and the relationship will take a bad turn.

Rejectees struggle with unconditional love most of their lives. If you didn't receive it when you were a child, you'll spend the rest of your life trying to get it from the people who may be unwilling or incapable of giving it to you.

This puts a lot of pressure on the person you have only been dating for a few weeks, and you want to be loved like nobody else has ever loved you before. When that person rejects your demands, you become needy and desperate. Picking up on that hungry dependence, the other person will flee the relationship.

People who have dependency issues are looking for unconditional love in all the wrong places. We've established that. So, the question becomes this:

"Where do I find this unconditional love?"

Just as you have to **choose yourself first**, so you can build trust, reliability, and confidence, and so do you have to **love yourself first**. Asking the world to give you this love is unrealistic. You will fail in holding these expectations for others.

Of course, we all need and desire love from other people, but depending on any one person completely to fill in that missing part of your life will lead to an emotional setback and eventually disappointment. But when we treat people we come into contact with each day with respect, admiration and appreciation, they will pick up on your positive attitude towards them.

As the **Dalai Lama** wisely expressed: *"If you want others to be happy, practice compassion. If you want to be happy, practice compassion."*

I have found no greater way to create unconditional love than to give away the best of myself at any given time. I know this sounds like a tall order, and it isn't always easy to just accept everyone, but try to open up your mind and heart as much as you can. Instead of desperately seeking that love you feel is missing, turn it around and realize that you have all that you need: It just has to be nurtured.

The one obstacle that holds people back is putting themselves in a position where they are vulnerable. We are afraid to just put ourselves out there in case we get injured or taken advantage of. But protecting ourselves is what we have been doing for a long time, and even though it feels natural and necessary to stray away from that rejection, by letting go of that fear of vulnerability, you are reducing the pain of going through a rejection.

How to Practice Unconditional Love

You want to experience unconditional love? Treat people without conditions. Do things for them without expecting anything. Say nice things about them and don't ask for anything in return. The moment you do something for someone and you attach a want or expectation to it, you are building that disappointment up again. Successful relationships are based on four important values:

- Mutual respect

- Valuing the people you are with

- Avoiding any form of harsh criticism

- Giving without heavy expectations

Relationships that are based on a give-and-take strategy don't experience the unconditional love that could be fostered if practicing these four simple principles. But the "I'll love you if you love me"—in any relationship, not just romantic—sets you up for failure.

As soon as one person decides that they're not sharing that love anymore, it's gone. Your unconditional-love pact has ended. You must wake up to this truth if you are going to get over this massive hurdle. It is time to accept that the unconditional love that you should have had as a kid most likely isn't going to happen.

One lesson I learned from having been through several dependency-type relationships is this: You can't get something from someone if they aren't willing or capable of sharing. Nobody can give you what he or she doesn't have. And the fact is, relying on someone to fulfill all of your needs isn't going to work out in the end.

If you have really deep issues around codependency, you might need a big push to get yourself to take action. You'll only be lovable when you can learn to give it away.

The cure isn't complicated—look at how you interact in relationships and take a moment to tap into your feelings. Are you being genuine, or putting up a front? Are you being completely open, or do you feel that you're hiding your true self for fear of being exposed? Are you interested in this relationship because of its potential, or is there an underlying motive?

Unconditional love is getting to that place where you can accept yourself completely, without illusions of perfectionism or feeding into the needy wants of a childhood ego. Unconditional love isn't what you have to have for everyone, but it is what you need for yourself and your children.

Many of our rejection-persona issues stem from childhood. They started there, and it is too late to go back and fix what was done. But you can start moving forward today.

Focus on loving yourself in a way that you never were as a child. Revisit your childhood and re-experience those feelings of shame, guilt, and rejection. Reach out to yourself and give the love that was withheld. Visualize yourself wanting these things as a child and not getting them. Walk yourself through the pain of those moments. Pull yourself back in if you try to escape. Stay focused on that memory and let it happen. See yourself wanting that approval and getting rejected for it.

Tapping into these memories brings up painful emotions. But these are the feelings that you have been escaping from most of your life. By avoiding what happened, you are keeping the lies that built this false persona. Exposing the truth and fully realizing that it was not your fault frees you from this pain over time.

Action Plan

Look for areas in your life where you expect love but you aren't getting it. Is it from your wife, husband, partner, or lover? How about your children? Do you have unrealistic demands? Are you needy or do you come across as demanding for love?

Focus on giving your love to someone in a way that you never received it. By this I don't mean romantic love, but genuine caring for other people. Because rejection is such a deep and painful issue, most people don't want to admit or even recognize that they have these issues. But you do. Everyone does to some extent, some more than others.

By helping others, you will create the opportunity to increase your personal value. I have found that by helping people, I naturally developed a deeper love for myself that was never there before. Trust me, if you like and respect yourself, you'll never have to worry about lack of love in your life.

If there is anything that can remove that fear of rejection, it is putting yourself out there, loving yourself more, and genuinely embracing the kindness of others. A lot of people out there need people like you. Don't let that "rejection bug" stop you from giving it.

Make a list of the things you feel ashamed or embarrassed about.

Is it...

• Being alone?

• Feeling jealous or envious of others?

• Wanting to be someone else instead of who you could be?

Take yourself through your emotions and observe how you are feeling. When we can identify the situations that trigger rejection, it puts us in a better position to take action. By knowing when you are experiencing a "rejection moment," you can put an end to that vicious cycle.

Chapter 8

Why We Fear Asking

"Rejection doesn't have to mean you aren't good enough; it often just means the other person failed to notice what you have to offer."

— **Ash Sweeney**

Asking for the things we want the most is one of the hardest things to do. We fear hearing that *NO* word more than any other word in the language.

Think back to when you were a kid. Chances are you asked for everything you could. When you didn't get it you became persistent and demanded it. If your parents said no (which they often did) you'd go away for a while but return later with a new plan of attack. You probably resorted to negotiating— "I'll clean my room for a week if you let me have what I want."

Eventually you either got what you wanted or you finally conceded that you had lost. You would pursue every avenue until what you wanted— that new toy or the latest cool gadget—was yours.

But over the years we change.

We start asking for less and end up taking what is available. We lose that hardline negotiating and whining that worked as kids. Our parents often told us to stop whining or being selfish, so we did. After all, nobody wants to be labeled as selfish.

This brings us to the **power of asking**, one of the core themes in this book, and a primary obstacle when it comes to facing rejection.

The fear of being rejected is what stops a rejectee from taking any kind of action. Instead of demanding or even asking, we lean toward acceptance and passive numbness. This is a path that leads to suffering. We suffer when we go without while watching others get what they want because they asked for it. You might develop resentment, not only towards those people who are "braver" than you but you'll label yourself as weak and a coward.

When you have to go without because you can't muster up the courage to ask for it—when we go without the things we crave, knowing that we could have them if we only stood up and did something—it hurts. We are buying into our own rejection and, in fact, creating more of it. You might avoid conflict or rejection by not asking, thinking you were spared the emotional pain of hearing *NO*, but the consequences of this are far worse in the long run.

In their groundbreaking and bestselling book, *The Aladdin Factor*, authors **Jack Canfield** and **Mark Victor Hansen** (*Chicken Soup for the Soul*) tell us that nothing comes without first making the decision that you deserve it, you want it, and you are going to have it. Then, knowing these facts, you seek out the right people who are going to help you to get it.

In this section, that is exactly what we are going to discuss: how to make a decision based on what you want, then figure out your plan for getting it.

Asking for the things that you want is one of the best strategies and habits for developing personal freedom. When you take a risk by asking for something, you open up huge doors for yourself. Opportunity doesn't come knocking and looking for takers; we have to forge the opportunity by stepping up, saying *YES*, and taking direct action. **Asking is the key to taking charge of your life**, and to the resulting success that follows.

The bottom line: **If you fail to ask, you fail to get.**

Here are some reasons we don't ask:

1.   The answer will be a definite *NO* (so why bother).

2. You will be embarrassed or humiliated if rejected.

3. You fear that if they say *YES,* you'll be expected to return the favor.

4. We undermine our own confidence, believing that we are not worthy to receive this.

5. Pride gets in the way when we associate asking with begging.

6. Low self-esteem issues: my needs are not that important and I can do without.

7. I might be judged for being poor for not having this already.

When you ask for something that you want, your confidence skyrockets and you prove to yourself that the fear you had was just an illusion keeping you trapped.

When you ask, you are desensitizing your fear of rejection. We will discuss desensitization more in the next section but, for now, know that developing the *asking habit* is the key to eliminating rejection fears.

For years I was too passive. I expected everything to just come my way, or that people would figure out what I wanted and give it to me without my asking.

But nobody knows better than you do what you want. People cannot read your mind. If you wait for someone to figure out what you want, and then hope they give it to you, you could be in for a long wait and a big setup for disappointment. This isn't patience; it is a form of self-denial.

If you knew all you had to do was ask, you could have everything you've ever wanted. But many people don't have what they want and they go without because they haven't asked for it.

Why? We believe that the answer will be *NO.* And hearing that word—*NO*—traces right back to childhood when we were denied the things we really wanted. Who denied us? Parents, teachers, and peers.

How many times have you been told, "Don't ask for it, because you're not getting it"? Fair enough—but regardless, we didn't get it; the want is still there. I can still recall things I wanted in my childhood and never got. Can you?

This sounds like such a simple concept. You ask for things all the time, right? But it's not the frequency of asking that matters. You have to ask for the right things.

If you ask for the wrong things all your life, any request will do. Why ask for oranges if you want apples? In other words, stop asking for the things you don't want or need.

There are three truths about asking:

1. People who ask for what they want usually get rejected.

2. People who don't ask for what they want never get rejected because they never ask.

3. People who keep asking for what they want may get rejected, but eventually they'll get what they want.

I concluded that, I could keep getting what I have always gotten. Or I could push myself to try and get the stuff I never imagined getting. When you ask for what you want and not what you think you're worth, it is like putting the key into the right door lock: You open up a whole new world of possibilities.

It follows a simple principal:

- Ask and you may receive.

- Don't ask and you'll never receive.

When I started asking for things, it all changed. I got some *NO*s; but I also got some people who said *YES*. And my averages were good. I received a *YES* about 60% of the time. If I hadn't asked for anything, I'd have gotten nothing. 60% works better than 0%.

Asking is paramount to succeeding. This is especially true when it comes to asking for help. I'll talk more on this later.

For years, I lived in hesitation because I feared the answer would confirm what I already believed: I wasn't worth it, and that's why I was constantly rejected.

This "asking action" changed the way I think about how to overcome my rejection addiction. Most of my life I shied away from asking for anything. I didn't want to get in the way or bother anyone. In other words, I didn't want to put myself in a position where I risked being rejected. If they said *NO*—and that was a very good possibility—it would reinforce every belief I had about myself that I was unworthy of getting the things I really wanted.

How will you know that you can have something if you never ask for it? By asking for what you want, you boost your chances of receiving this exponentially. If you don't ask for it, your chances of getting nothing would be almost guaranteed. Nobody is going to read your mind; they don't know what you want, and even if they did, would they just offer it to you? Most likely not.

Years ago, I stopped asking for what I wanted out of fear that I would leave myself open to vulnerability, I would owe somebody something that I could never repay, or they would see me as weak or needy. My pride would get in the way.

There are so many things that I have wanted in my life that I never received for one reason only. It wasn't lack of money or skill; it was the absence of courage to ask for what I desired most.

Not asking for what you want because of the fear of looking stupid, feeling powerless, being humiliated—those are all fears of rejection. You learned at a young age that is it better to just take what you can get instead of risking everything by asking for what you want. You don't want to appear needy or helpless.

There is a price to pay for not asking. You might avoid the humiliation of being rejected, but by avoiding asking for the stuff you really want, you will lose a lot more. By trading in your pride and fear of embarrassment, you could be giving up large sums of money (asking for a raise), your freedom (asking for time off), and the opportunity to thrive instead of survive.

Here is a list of reasons why asking counts:

- If you don't ask for directions, you end up going the wrong way

- If you don't ask for financial assistance to go back to school, you can't get a good education and you end up unemployed, possibly permanently

- If you don't ask to borrow someone's car because yours broke down and you need to get to work, you miss a day's pay and the manager is not happy

- If you don't ask that person out on a date, someone else will

- If you don't ask for more money in your work, you'll have less money

- If you don't ask for support, you end up doing it alone

- If you don't ask how it's done, you'll end up doing it the wrong way

- If you don't ask for an extension on that deadline, you'll be up late tonight trying to get it all done

- If you don't ask for time off, you work harder and risk burning out

- If you don't ask the waiter to heat up your dinner more because you want it hotter, you end up paying full price for an expensive meal that's cold

- If you don't ask your spouse to listen to you when you have something important to say, then you end up unfulfilled, unhappy, and resentful

- If you don't ask for a second chance, you have to accept your first attempt as a painful lesson in failing

By not asking, you are taking a big risk. You are making a decision to be less, have less, and ultimately to want less. You will eventually make excuses for yourself and say, "Oh that's okay, I didn't really need it anyway."

Really? You don't want help with something? You don't want more money for your hard work or more time off? You don't want more friends or people who will listen to you? You don't want more confidence? You don't want a discount on your hotel room? You don't want to go out with that girl that lives down the street, even though she's been looking at you every morning as you jogged by? You don't want a bank loan to buy a new house?

I don't believe it.

And neither should you.

Selling yourself short is telling the world "I'm not worthy of any of these things, so I won't ask for anything." If that's the case, you'll end up shorthanded and short changed. You'll get what others give you. And what they give you could be the remains of the good stuff they are finished with.

When you don't ask for the things that you truly desire, there is always somebody else that will. While you are busy waiting for someone to give you what you secretly want, others are pushing ahead, asking, and receiving their gifts.

The Risk Worth Taking

If you could ask for what you wanted from this day on, where would you start? What would you ask for first?

Make a list of all the stuff you have been holding out on. Would you ask for help with a project? Would you approach the bank and apply for a loan so you can start that business? Would you ask for better benefits at work? Would you reach out to your friend for help, or a stranger?

Make a list of all the things that would improve your situation drastically. Here are some ideas:

- What would you ask for at home?

- What about when you go out in public? Would you ask someone to move their car so you could squeeze into the next parking spot?

- What would you ask for at a restaurant? A café? A shopping mall?

- Would you ask for a price reduction on older items in a shop?

- Would you ask a stranger to have coffee?

- Would you ask someone to loan you money on the promise that you would return it within a specified time frame?

- Would you ask someone to treat you with more respect and stop criticizing?

The power of asking is one of the key components to really kicking your fear of rejection out of your life. You can numb your fear by taking action and doing something every day that desensitizes you to this fear.

Asking is equated to taking risk. But it is **a good risk**. It's the risk that gets you out of a rut and puts you in greater control of your life. You feel powerful and centered. By asking, you are taking charge of your life. That fear of being rejected is reduced to a minuscule whimper. Eventually you won't even feel it anymore.

Now that is something worth having.

If it is true that, by asking, you get what you ask for, you also deprive yourself of the things you don't ask for.

Don't ask and you won't get; ask once and you might get it. Ask again and again and you'll increase your chances of getting anything exponentially!

That's how simple it is.

At the very least, by asking for what you want and putting yourself out there, you'll build up a tough resistance to hearing *NO*. The more you hear *NO*, the easier it becomes. You will desensitize yourself to being told to bugger off.

"Recognizing that you are not where you want to be is a starting point to begin changing your life."

— Deborah Day

When you ask and someone looks at you with doubt and you know they won't comply with your request, instead of feeling that pang of anxiety that says "Ouch, I've been told *NO* again," you'll develop a tougher skin for getting told *NO*. Instead of fearing rejection, you will come to embrace you.

In his bestselling novel *Rejection Proof,* author **Jia Jiang** put rejection to the test. For one hundred days he put himself in situations where he asked for literally anything, often very absurd stuff that people would certainly say *NO* to. Several times he was shocked that he actually got a *YES* and was given the opportunity to try something he normally would never have thought of.

By putting himself in situations in which he was almost guaranteed to fail, he desensitized himself to getting told *NO*. After one hundred days he had more freedom than he had ever experienced.

As Jiang experienced through this experiment, you won't be cured by getting rejected once, but by doing it continuously. It acts as a major boost of confidence and pushes the power of rejection right out the door. We will discuss this more in section 3, but as the experiments in rejection have proven, you only earn your freedom and break those "chains" when you get out there and do it.

For years, I asked for nothing unless I absolutely had to. If it was something I needed and couldn't do without, and I was in a position where asking another human being was the only way, I'd do it. But only in extreme circumstances. I was like a silent watchdog that always had my eye on things I desired but stayed in the shadows and watched, while others moved ahead by taking action.

For years I made excuses for not asking. I would say things like …

"I can figure it out for myself."

"Oh no, don't trouble yourself. I'll take care of it."

"It's not important."

"I'll ask tomorrow."

If this is you, let's take action to change this. Don't be a silent watchdog and suffer without. You deserve to have everything you have ever wanted.

You deserve it no matter what your mind tells you.

Chapter 9

Essentials to Asking for What You Want

"Everyone at some point in life have faced rejection and failure, it is part of the process to self-realization."

— **Lailah Gifty Akita**

H ere are the eight steps you can use for asking for anything you want. This will be hard in the beginning, but after putting yourself out there and doing it, you'll get the hang of it. Soon you'll be asking for everything without second guessing yourself.

The 8 Steps to Getting to YES

Step 1: STOP thinking about the negative outcome, which is getting rejected and hearing *NO*. It doesn't matter, because if you don't ask, you're rejecting yourself and you won't get anything anyway. You have created a lose-lose situation before you've begun. Focusing on a bad outcome is going to affect the way you ask, if you do at all.

By expecting to be refused, you'll go into the situation lacking any confidence at all. People are much more apt to give you something if you act like you really deserve it. If you show fear or you are already dreading that first *NO*, it will show. If you are focused on the outcome not turning out the way you want it to, turn it around so that you visualize yourself getting that *YES*.

Step 2: Visualize the action of ASK, not the response—it is not important that you get a *YES*. Of course, that is what you want, but if you bank everything on getting that *YES* and you keep getting told *NO*, you'll revert back to thinking about the negative outcome. The positive outcome is the action of you asking. Not the result. You have been so focused on the response that you forget it is the courage that we had to conjure up to ask in the first place that is the real victory. Forget about the outcome. Focus on the action of asking. You can do this by **visualizing** yourself doing it.

See yourself opening that door and walking into a room. The person that stands between you and what you desire is sitting there in a chair in the center of that room. Imagine walking right up to him or her and asking for that one thing you have always wanted. Now, take it a step further and see them reacting to your request.

You can run through various outcomes; would they get angry and start shouting, or smile and just say, "Sure, you can have that. Why didn't you ask me sooner?" I used this technique a lot when I struggled with asking. I still do. Visualizing yourself doing it is a powerful approach to psyching up your courage, and it actually gets you excited about doing this. You'll be less fearful and anxious.

Step 3: Ask yourself, "What is the worst that could possibly happen?" Rejection is a game of deception. When you visualize yourself taking a risk or moving toward something that sets off fear, the feeling is like drowning. You think you won't survive, and that death is near.

But let's get practical: What is the worst that could possibly happen? You have to remind yourself that life will go on. You'll live through it. You have nothing to lose (except pride and ego) so why not? If you don't ask, you lose anyway.

We often attach a disaster to the outcome as if, by getting a rejection, it is the end of everything. This fear is centered in the belief that we can't handle it. *"If they turn me down my life is forfeit."* I can tell you that life will go on, and the great thing is, you'll develop a mental toughness for it.

Step 4: Understand that rejection is an illusion. It is the ultimate lie that keeps you trapped. As long as you believe that you have everything to lose, you will be paralyzed with fear to do anything. I convince my subconscious mind that rejection doesn't exist, accept in my own mind.

Sure, we do get brushed aside, turned down, and told that we just aren't good enough. But that is the journey that successful people take. If you let a single rejection stop you from persisting, you'll struggle throughout your life to make anything work.

The power of the illusion is as strong as you decide it to be. You can let it defeat you or accept it into your life as part of the growing process.

Step 5: Keep on asking. Success is in the numbers: the more you ask, the better you get at it. It is a skill you can master with practice. You might only get one *YES* out of every fifty rejections, but it's better than nothing. And nothing is what you'll get if you don't ask.

Keep in mind that timing has a lot to do with your success rate. There were times I asked people for something once and they said *NO*; but when I asked again they agreed. Were they having a bad day when I asked the first time? Maybe they didn't need what I was offering at that time?

Persistence pays. Believe in what you are going for and ask with conviction. This will boost your chances of succeeding.

Step 6: Know WHO to ask and stop complaining about not having what you want. There is no point in asking a person who is unemployed for a job; they can't give you what they don't have. You have to ask the right people. What this means is, don't waste your time asking the people who have nothing to do with what you are going after. In addition, complaining to others about your hard fortune and not having what you desire will just perpetuate your situation of having less.

For a long time, I had a bad habit of complaining to friends and anyone who would listen about how I was always missing out. If someone I knew succeeded because they took the initiative and went after their goals (most likely by doing a lot of asking) I would be hit with jealousy and complain about how lucky he or she was. Luck had nothing to do with it.

The bottom line: stop complaining. You have no reason to complain and it can only do you more harm while building a wall of resentment. If you aren't taking action to get what you want, you can only blame yourself.

Step 7: Know WHEN to ask. Your timing can have a lot to do with the outcome of your asking moment. You wouldn't want to ask someone for a favor if they were in the middle of a personal crisis. For one thing, they are maybe not in a position to help you at that moment, or that particular time of day there is just too much going on. Observe and take notes. Know what you want to ask for and then watch for the opportune moment.

The most powerful approach is to do it with empathy. When possible, observe their situation and seek to understand the other person's emotions and feelings at the time. This could be challenging in a business environment, but every situation has its unique approach.

For example, how you ask your spouse for something would be different than asking a co-worker or manager. The level of empathy is different as well, but by measuring the situation and approaching when the timing feels right can deliver a better outcome.

Step 8: Know WHAT to ask for. One of the biggest reasons people go without is because they don't know what they want in the first place. You have to be clear about what it is you want, or you'll end up asking for the wrong things; or worse yet, you'll just take what anyone is giving away.

Remember: People normally don't want to give you what you want, especially if they still want to keep it, or what you are asking for is going to cost them in some way. But knowing WHAT you want will also determine WHO to ask. On the list of you made at the beginning of all the stuff you are going to ask for, now go back and fill in the name or names of the people who can give it to you.

Who can you reach out to today? Is there one person above all the rest that can deliver on what you want to have? Then you know what to do. But you might be having second thoughts. You are thinking they'll turn you down, or worse.

Chapter 10

Simple Strategies for Asking

*"Rejection can disappoint you, depress you and may even
stop you in your tracks... learn not to take rejection so
personally... if you're honest with yourself and believe in
your work, others will too."*

— **Bev Jozwiak**

Now, make a list of twenty things you are going to ask for today.
Who are you going to ask? When? How much will you ask for?
Be sure to be specific about what you want. Just "asking for time off"
from your work isn't specific enough. You have to ask for three days or
three weeks. Be sure that what you are asking for is **what you really
want** and that it is **specific**.

When you go to the bank to apply for a loan, you don't just say, "Give
me some cash for a car." You need to state how much it is you need.

Be **specific**.

Be **clear**.

Be **confident**.

Now, here are the nine strategies you can put into action when asking:

1. Keep track of your asking score.

Here is a tactic you can use when procrastinating on doing something. A friend of mine would keep two jars: one full of pennies and the other empty. When he took a positive action, such as completing a simple task or asking for something, he would move one penny to the empty jar. It worked because that simple action of moving pennies prompted him to do something every day. He said that he wanted to see how many pennies he could fill up the empty jar with.

Make a challenge with yourself and start off the beginning of the month with two jars, one empty and the other filled with thirty coins (or jellybeans or whatever you wish). Then everyday make a goal to ask for one thing you want. It doesn't have to be anything extravagant. Regardless if you get a *YES* or *NO*, you still win. The victory is in getting to the "ask" stage. Beyond that, the outcome doesn't matter.

2. It's a give-and-give some more.

When I learned to ask more and could confidently approach people about my desires to own, be, or do something, I had a great moment of clarity. When I received, I didn't just want to get more and keep taking. This isn't what asking is all about. You have to be willing to give as much as you earn, and even more. There will come a time in your life that people will ask you for the things you want.

I realized that what I received I was also willing to give away; but when I was rejected, or when I rejected myself by holding on to my "ask," I was less willing and kind to share with others. My rejectionism had created a level of scarcity in me that made me unwilling to give. I held on tightly and constructed a barrier around my life. Asking was another path to freedom and it can be yours too.

3. Believe you're worth receiving it.

For many years I shied away from asking for what I wanted. The reason was, I didn't think I was worthy of having it. Lacking confidence and low self-esteem, I would either take what was given to me, or learned to live with what I had. When you ask for something, you have to believe that it's yours to begin with. If you don't believe in it then who will?

One of the reasons we get turned down is because our approach is weak. If you are lacking confidence it shows in your attitude. You can't fake it. You are more likely to make a good case if you can trust in yourself that it is yours.

4. Develop an attitude of gratitude for what you get.

This isn't the same as "Settle for what you get." But the reality is, you might ask for ten dollars and receive five. You ask for a week off and you get five days. You ask for a kiss and you get a handshake.

We have to appreciate the fact that what we want isn't what people are always willing to offer up right away. Patience is part of the game, and if you lose your patience or turn from asking to demanding, you could end up losing everything.

5. Visualize your "big ask."

Visualization is a powerful technique that can prepare your mind for what it is going to do. It is so powerful that athletes, negotiators and presidents visualize the success they want to achieve and the outcome before taking action. Visualization is your mind training for taking action in the near future. If you can envision it, you can have it. Or at the very least, you can prompt your mind into taking action.

World-renowned actor and comedian **Jim Carrey** improvised a powerful visualization technique when he was struggling as an actor in Hollywood. In 1985, Carrey, with dreams of becoming a famous actor in Hollywood, wrote himself a check for 10 million dollars for "acting services rendered." He kept it in his wallet postdated for ten years. Carrey later went on to be paid millions for huge blockbuster films such as *Ace Ventura*, *Liar Liar* and *The Cable Guy*.

6. Visualize the engagement as a positive experience.

When I tried this for the first time, I would visualize the other person as becoming confrontational and angry. This created intense emotions of stress and anger. So, even when I did get up the courage to ask, I did it in a very aggressive manner. I wasn't asking but demanding. The other person, sensing this hostility, reacted in a similar state.

Under these circumstances, even if you get what you want, you'll damage your relationship with that person and kill any chances of future "win-win" situations. You might get what you want but at a price.

Visualize your "asking moment" as a positive, calm approach to the situation. It might not turn out the way you want it but going in with guns blazing is a sure way to kill any negotiations.

7. Know you have nothing to lose.

When you are gearing up to ask or approach someone, always tell yourself that you have nothing to lose: there is only a gain, even if you come away with a *NO*. Asking for things is like any other skill: it improves over time. The more you do it the better at it you get. You can only lose out by not asking.

One of the obstacles that creates hesitation and prevents us from taking action is the distorted belief that, if we are turned down, it'll feel worse than death, as if we have lost something vitally important. But, as I have stated, there is nothing to lose if you take courage and do something about it.

8. Know that the rejection begins in your mind.

Most of how we respond is based on our self-perception and understanding of the situation. If you get rejected, you can make it all about you and tell yourself it's because you are no good, worthless, and deserved to be rejected because you are unworthy. The other way to look at it is to see this as a moment where the person isn't ready to accept your offer; they are not ready yet, regardless of how badly or how much you beg.

People change day to day. What they want one day isn't what they desire the next. If you take rejection personally you are setting yourself up for future suffering. The rejection you labeled it as is all in your mind. You have to choose yourself in these moments and realize there will be other opportunities and circumstances to ask someone else.

9. Project your confidence.

You will have a much better chance of succeeding if you ask with confidence. Ask as if you really mean it and that you have already gotten a *YES*. People who lack confidence appear as if they don't really want what they are trying to get. The requestee picks up on this and is less likely to agree with your terms.

You can deliver this confidence before you even say anything. Pay attention to your body language, eye contact, and voice control. Do you sound confident? Do you look confident? Do you smell confident (people can "smell" fear)? Project the attitude of confidence with self-talk before you do anything. Pump yourself up and remind yourself there is nothing to lose.

You Get What You Ask For

When I was in college I had an interview for a part-time job on the weekends working on a construction site. In the interview the owner had asked me, "So if we hire you, how much do you expect to be paid?" I didn't want to risk not getting hired by asking for too much, even though I knew the work would be hard, so I gave a price just above minimum wage. I was hired and paid the price I asked for, which at the time was just above $6 per hour. I felt pretty good about that because I had negotiated my wages and the manager had accepted.

Several weeks later I found out that one of the other workers, who had been hired right after me, was getting nearly $2 more an hour! I approached the owner to ask why I was being treated so unfairly even though we were both doing the same job. He simply said, "I asked you how much you wanted. We are paying you what you asked for. The other guy is also getting what he asked for."

This was a powerful lesson that stayed with me for years to come.

You always get what you ask for. When it comes to the subject of rejection, as you already know, most of us will do anything to avoid getting turned down, even if it means devaluing ourselves. Another lesson to learn is not only will you get what you ask for in life, but what you don't ask for you'll get as well … and that usually means nothing!

If you wait around for others to figure out what you want, you'll go without the things you really desire. Meanwhile, those that get ahead are seizing the moment and asking again and again and again for what they believe they deserve to have.

There is a saying: "Good things come to those who wait." I think this statement has a negative meaning—you might wait patiently for your day to arrive, for the right person to show up with the right opportunity, but it will come at a price. You could end up getting what is left over by those people who got there before you. "The early bird gets the worm" is a better expression to live by.

Think about all the things you are not asking for in your life. Chances are you could fill up a page right now. So that is what we are going to do, right now. Take out a piece of paper and make a list of all the things you want to ask for but have been afraid to. This can be anything from stuff at work to family issues.

Here are some prompts to get you moving:

- *"What am I afraid to ask my spouse?"*

- *"What am I afraid to ask my co-workers?"*

- *"What am I afraid to ask total strangers?"*

- *"What am I afraid to ask my neighbors?"*

- *"What am I afraid to ask my teachers?"*

- *"What am I afraid to ask of myself?"*

Everyone has something they are afraid to ask for. Once you clearly identify the things you are afraid to ask for, you can move forward with the next phase:

"Why?"

Next to the list of things you are afraid to ask for, write down the reason why you are afraid to ask. This is the fuel that will move you into taking action. Knowing what you are afraid to ask for is the first step because it makes you aware of what you are hiding from. But the *why* should make you at least a little angry.

Chapter 11

Asking for Help

"Rejection is merely a redirection; a course correction to your destiny.

— **Bryant McGill**

When it comes to asking for help, there is a certain level of resistance that stands between you and the person you are reaching out to. When you ask another person to help you, you are leaving yourself completely vulnerable. It feels like you are giving the other party permission to take full advantage of you. How terrifying!

What if they say *NO*? What if they tell you that you're just not good enough to be helped? These sound like crazy responses to a reasonable request ("Hey, would you mind giving me a hand?") but rejection plays crazy games with the mind.

When you ask for help, especially for men, there is that stigma that says asking for help is the equivalent of admitting you can't do something. When you admit you can't do something it is the same as saying "I can't handle it." You might equate asking for help with being weak or incompetent.

But that's just not the case. Everybody needs help with something. And most people need help every day, but they won't ask for it. I can remember walking around in the large city of Tokyo once, looking for a certain spot. When it was obvious how lost I was, I had no other choice but to stop someone and ask for directions. Before I did, this is what was going through my mind:

What if they don't stop?

What if they laugh?

What if they say, "Sorry, can't help you."

It sounds over-the-top, but this is how the rejectee thinks. We run through a list of possible scenarios that lead to the worst-case scenario in every situation. And it always comes back to the same thing: "What if I get rejected? It will shatter me."

So, what did I do?

I did ask someone. The first person didn't stop. The next person I asked did. Not only did they tell me where the place was, they went out of their way to show me personally right to the front door.

Where would I have ended up if I hadn't asked? Lost and confused and kicking myself for not asking.

Asking for help, as terrifying as it can seem, is perfectly natural. In fact, when I think about it, I was always happy in any situation to lend a hand myself when someone needed help. It was a chance to be of service to another human being. By giving, you will receive every time, and if you don't receive anything, you are still ahead of the game.

You see, I was always afraid of asking anyone for anything. If I needed help with something, I would figure out a way so that I didn't have to ask. If someone saw me struggling, I would tell him or her, "It's okay, I got this." But the reality is, I wanted their help; I just couldn't admit it. I was always terrified that if I accepted help from someone, I would owe him or her something, and I'd never be able to pay it back. I didn't want to appear needy or incompetent.

So, go ahead and ask someone for help. Better yet, offer to help someone if it looks like they need help. Not everyone will ask for it and may even refuse it if you try to give it to them.

Here are some things you can start with:

- Ask someone to help you fix your car.

- Ask someone to help you lift something.

- Ask someone to help you with your homework.

- Ask someone to help you solve a difficult problem.

- Ask someone to show you the way to the hotel because you're lost.

- Ask someone to lend you some money because you forgot your wallet today.

- Ask someone to help you carry something heavy.

So, what help are you going to ask someone to help you with?

Now, it is up to you.

Draft up twenty ideas of things to ask for this week. You can also reflect on last week and come up with ideas on things you could have asked for but didn't. Chances are they will come up again.

One more exercise you can try is a self-analysis practice. Look at areas of your life that you are terrified to approach. This could be in a relationship, or a situation at work. Maybe you can't handle asking people for help no matter what. You fear looking stupid. Take note of the areas you retreat from.

Then …

Choose one of your fears and focus on it. Think about how you are going to ask for this one thing. Feel the fear as it works its way through you. How will you ask for this? Who will you ask? When will you ask?

So, here is my simple 6-step process for asking for what you want:

1. Write down in a notebook or Evernote the one thing you really want.

2. Make a short list of three people who could provide this.

3. Write down the benefit you are providing by asking them for what you desire to have.

4. Ask confidently, as if it is already yours.

5. Be respectful of their decision if it doesn't turn out the way you wanted.

6. Finally, let go of your expectations.

You can make a massive difference in your life by asking the right people for the right things at the right time. Commit to asking for at least one thing you desire once a day. This can be something you want for yourself, or better yet, help someone else to obtain something they want.

Nothing happens in life unless you really want it. If you want it, you have to get out there and tell people. We can do this by asking for what is important.

Now, think very carefully about the one thing you want right now but you're holding back on asking for it. How are you going to ask? Who are you going to ask? When are you going to ask? To make it happen there has to be a plan. You need to decide what, where, and who. When you know this half, the work is already finished.

Create a Benefits Chart: Why Asking Pays

Create a benefits chart. On one side, you are going to list the benefits of not asking. On the other side, list the gains of asking. This is your **win-win** chart. Measure up both sides and see just how rejection is keeping you stuck.

What you can do is write down exactly what you want to ask for, and then how you are going to do it. How will you ask? What will you say? When will you ask for this? Interview yourself and get pumped up and excited about asking for the things you deserve and desire.

Chapter 12

Desensitization and the Flooding Process

"When you're not putting yourself out there, you're rejecting yourself by default."

— **Jia Jiang,** bestselling author of
Rejection Proof

Y ou think you are protecting yourself when you avoid situations that are potentially harmful to your ego, confidence and pride. In fact, what appears as a protective cocoon really ends up becoming a personal prison created not to protect you but to isolate your fear from experiencing what it needs to in order to step out of the way.

In this final section of the book we are taking a look at how desensitization works and how to put it into action so you can numb your fear of getting rejected.

In *psychology*, **desensitization** is defined as *'the diminished emotional responsiveness to a negative or aversive stimulus after repeated exposure to it.* It also occurs when an emotional response is repeatedly *evoked in situations in which the action tendency that is associated with the emotion proves irrelevant or unnecessary.*

Jia Jiang and 100 Days of Rejection

Could you imagine putting yourself into a state of **Rejection Proof** where, for 100 days, you committed to provoking rejection in order to numb yourself to its negative effects? This is what Jia Jiang did in his Rejection Journey. Dubbed the "Rejection Whisperer," Jiang put himself on a quest to intentionally get rejected for 100 days as a way to overcome rejection by throwing himself right at it again and again.

Ever since he was little, Jia Jiang fantasized about being an entrepreneur. After getting a rejection email from a potential investor for one of his inventions that would launch his entrepreneur business, Jiang set out to "thrive in the face of fear," as he said. And the experiment was on. For the next 100 days, recording each attempt with his phone, Jiang tried some pretty crazy experiments in his attempt to get rejected.

Some of the best ways he would try to get rejected were:

- Asking a security guard for $100

- Asking to be allowed to make an announcement over the PA system at Costco

- Asking a hairstylist if he could cut her hair

- Asking a donut shop if he could have a special donut in the shape of the Olympic rings

- Be a tour guide at a museum

- Sell cookies for the Girl Scouts

- Find a job in one day

- Be a greeter at Starbucks

- Get a hair trim at PetSmart

- Challenge a CEO to a staring contest

What is important about Jia Jiang's social experiment on rejection isn't the fact that he did something that has rarely been done before, but that he changed and evolved from doing it. He learned with each lesson and attempt at getting rejected.

The lesson Jiang shares is critical to understanding *why* people reject you. You see, when you have a situation where you get turned down, told *NO*, or basically given bad news that you just aren't good enough for the "team," it feels like a personal invasion on your character. Think about the last time you experienced a really bad rejection. If you are like me it was like being stabbed repeatedly, but on an emotional scale.

In his book *Rejection Proof*, Jiang explains:

> *"I'd always viewed my rejection as some sort of rare disease like guinea worm, that inflicts terrible pain but only affects a tiny segment of the population."*

I can relate and I am sure you can too. But isn't it true that when you are experiencing some form of rejection, whether it be personal or in business, somehow it feels like it's all about you? That somehow there is something about you in particular that caused this and that nobody else is going through anything even remotely similar?

Let's look at it another way. If you perform for a musical audition and there are 500 performers, only one person is going to be chosen. It might be you and it might not be, but regardless, 499 people will be getting turned down. The same goes for interviews, dating, and sending in a book for submission to a publisher. Someone is going to get rejected. It's a relief to know that it isn't just you.

Jia Jiang also says:

> *"Outside influences have an enormous impact on the way people see a situation-- and those influences can change over time. The way someone feels about me, or about a request I'm making, can be impacted by factors that have nothing to do with me. If people's behaviors and opinions can change so drastically based on so many factors, why should I take everything about a rejection so personally?"*

We are sensitive people by nature. And rejection is the virus that has heightened that sensitivity to a boiling point. The fear we have that is labeled "fear of rejection" is really a deep and personal fear of ourselves. How "I" feel after getting rejected is ten times worse than what other people are thinking. But when it happens, shame kicks in. This, attached to a highly sensitive individual, makes everything that happens personal.

But as Jiang says, there are so many variables and reasons for not getting accepted that are way beyond our control. Beautiful, highly intelligent, rich, and powerful individuals struggle with the same thing. People who we look at and think "She has nothing to worry about" based on her appearance or social status.

But it comes back to this: I have yet to meet a perfect individual who was capable of getting everything they want or being liked by everyone. The next time you think so, check to see if they have wings on their backs, because everyone is vulnerable.

Everyone has defects. But we learn to deal with them. And, by focusing on personal development as a way to always make progress, you can combat your feelings of inadequacy. If you get rejected for something, you could ask for feedback as to *why* you received a *NO*.

By getting feedback and understanding more the reason for the decision, you can use that information to focus on tightening up a weak spot. I wouldn't go out and get plastic surgery if someone doesn't like the way I look, but, if it is a skill I can improve on such as public speaking, there are always ways to make it better.

You might feed these lies to yourself:

- *"I was rejected because I'm ugly."*

- *"I was rejected because I'm not smart enough for this."*

- *"I was rejected because I can't be loved."*

The list of lies goes on. But none of them are true.

So how do we get to the point in our lives where we can move beyond this illusion and start to feel better about who we are?

You already know the answer. From the beginning of this book we discussed how to choose yourself above any situation; how to tackle tough moments where failure was imminent and how to ask for what you want as a way of breaking that barrier.

But here is the thing. It isn't the fear of people that is the problem. For years I always thought that people were the problem, and if I could just figure them out I'd be less fearful of criticism and judgment. But it wasn't that.

Rejection rarely has anything to do with anyone else and more to do with how we feel about ourselves. As Jiang said, the judgments and decisions people make are based on their feelings, attitude, needs, and wants in the moment. If you don't have what they are looking for they'll find someone who does.

Understanding this one concept cuts our fear in half. When you look at it this way, you could say that rejection doesn't actually exist. It is a self-created condition that is rarely controlled by anyone else except yourself.

Chapter 13

Getting Desensitized to Rejection

"There are two wrong reactions to a rejection slip: deciding it's a final judgment on your story and/or talent and deciding it's no judgment on your story and/or talent."

— Nancy Kress

When I finished high school, I had a job in construction and most of the work we did was outside. In the winter the temperature dropped to about minus fifteen or twenty. Those are cold conditions to be spending six hours a day outdoors working. But after a few days you got used to it. The first couple of days feeling that cold was intense, but over the course of a few days you never thought about it.

You'll get used to the conditions you are exposed to over a certain period of time and your body will condition itself to adverse situations after a certain length of exposure. Even today, nearly twenty years later, the cold doesn't bother me as much as most people I know. My exposure to harsh temperatures toughened up my mindset toward adverse conditions.

The same principle works for most things we fear, including rejection. We fear what we least understand, and if you are struggling with your personal rejectee issues, it is because you have been avoiding placing yourself in the path of direct fire. In other words, what we run from doesn't disappear; it just buries itself deeper. That which you resist, persists.

Facing and defeating rejection works in a similar way. You can reduce its power by conditioning yourself through exposure to rejection. This is what it means to desensitize yourself.

Desensitizing yourself to the fear of rejection is about taking action toward the events or situations that you fear the most.

Desensitization is practiced through conditioning your mind with repeated attempts at getting rejected. Based on respondent conditioning, it is a form of behavioral therapy used by psychiatrists to help people overcome deep fears and phobias. Also known as **flooding**, this type of practice can be used to condition yourself for rejection.

As we discussed earlier, **Jia Jiang** gives an amazing account of how he put himself out there to purposely get rejected over the course of one hundred days. His purpose was to get so used to being rejected that he no longer felt anything about it.

There is a lesson to be learned here that states: **What we do repeatedly becomes second nature.**

This could also be called **rejection mastery**. You get so used to it that soon it is no longer an issue.

Another interesting experiment that I tested is called Rejection Therapy, a systematic approach to mastering rejection originally created by entrepreneur **Jason Comely**. The rules of the game go like this:

You must be rejected by one person at least once a day. To be specific, you have to be rejected, not just try to be, but to do something that gets you turned down. If you get out there and give it a shot but your attempt at rejection fails, it doesn't count. Getting rejected is SUCCESS in this Rejection Therapy game. If your rejection is accepted, you can take it that you didn't ask for enough.

Can you imagine how you would feel after thirty days if you purposely put yourself in a position that challenged your comfort zone and pushed your fear of being told *NO* to the very edge? This is what desensitization is all about. You have been buying into rejection because, like many people, you spent your life trying to avoid it. By hiding from it and protecting yourself, you become weaker, not stronger.

Don't you think it's time to do something about this? I know I do.

What you can do right now is make a list of all the crazy ways you can get rejected. This can be a simple request; start out small if you want to. Build up to it. Let yourself get desensitized in small steps each day. Every day try and push the envelope a little further. See how many ideas you can come up with.

Then, at the start of each morning, choose the one you are going to implement today. You can make up your own rules for this, too. You can do it the Rejection Therapy way and count it as a success only IF you get rejected, or you can give yourself credit for trying it regardless of the outcome.

Creating Your Own Rejection Challenge

What ideas can you come up with to desensitize and reduce your fear of rejection?

Here are some things I have tried:

- I went to a computer shop and asked if I could borrow a computer for the weekend because mine had broken. Result: They said no, but that I could buy a second-hand computer for a very low price (at their store of course).

- I asked someone I didn't know if I could stay at their house for a week because mine was being renovated. Result: They said *NO* but offered to help me find a cheap hotel.

- I asked the police if I could take a ride with them in the patrol car. Result: They said *NO* but that if I went to the station and filed a request it would probably be granted. I didn't do that because I knew it was a no-brainer, but I asked something I never would have tried before playing the game.

- I went to an all-female Yoga studio and asked to join up. Result: They said *NO* (of course) but did direct me to a Yoga studio for men and women.

Challenge Your Rejection

Now, why don't you challenge yourself to giving it a try. See how many situations you can come up with where you are putting yourself in a situation with the possibility of being rejected.

Here are 10 fun challenges you can start with:

1. Approach ten people at random and complement each of them. This can be about something they are wearing, their style of haircut, or a personal characteristic you noticed.
2. Go to a furniture store and ask if you can take a twenty-minute power nap on one of their model beds.
3. Meet with your employer or boss at work and ask him or her if you can finish working thirty minutes earlier from now on to spend more time at home with family.
4. Tell someone it's your birthday, and ask him or her to sing Happy Birthday to you.
5. In a supermarket or café, ask if you can "skip to the front of the line" because you are "patience intolerant."
6. The next time you check in for a flight, ask to be upgraded to first class without paying extra.
7. Challenge someone to a staring contest. You have to hold the stare for a minimum of one minute.
8. Ask your manager or the CEO of the company if you can work in their office for the day because you feel it will help you become more productive.
9. Draw a picture. This can be anything. You can add color to it or make it as creative as you like. Then, carry it around for the day and whenever you meet someone, show him or her the drawing and ask, "So, what do you think?"
10. Ask a random couple on the street to tell you the story of how they met.

Chapter 14

No More Excuses

"Just get out there and get rejected, and sometimes it's going to get dirty. But that's OK, 'cause you're going to feel great after, you're going to feel like, 'Wow. I disobeyed fear.' "

— **Jason Comely**

You need to take some small risk of the ego or else you'll stay where you are. If you don't, you'll have nobody to blame but yourself. Small steps make real progress over time. Taking no steps keeps you stuck. Even if you make small progress every day, it's still better than the other 99% of the people out there who are doing nothing.

Most people talk about the things they want to do, and they end up making excuses as to why they can't do them. Excuses are another way we keep ourselves trapped. You can free yourself by throwing out outdated reasoning that feeds the lies of what you can or cannot do.

- *"I'll do it when I have enough time ..."*

- *"I'll do it when I save more money ..."*

- *"I'll do it after I finish school ..."*

- *"I'll do it when the kids are gone ..."*

But those "some days" never come, and in the end, they live meager lives and forsake their dreams, casting aside everything for the hope of something that never comes.

Your excuses will reinforce the chances of getting rejected. We make excuses because we fear negative consequences.

- *"What if it doesn't work out?"*

- *"What if they don't approve my application?"*

- *"What if I don't finish what I started?"*

- *"What if I get stuck?"*

- *"What if I fail?"*

I have always strived to make a better life for myself, but along the road I got stuck many times. I stayed stuck for many years, stuck in jobs, wasting time in dead-end relationships, hooked into various addictions, and spending my life like someone who didn't care very much for themselves. I wasn't just killing time, but I was killing myself, and my life.

The bottom line: **You owe yourself to live BIG.** There is no satisfaction in living small and staying hidden from the world. You can put yourself out there by choosing who you want to be and accepting who you presently are.

There are no more lies or illusions when you decide to take charge of your life.

When you choose to NOT believe in the lies, you are taking affirmative action toward an inner healing. You stop playing the victim and take charge. You can only do this if you make a conscious decision to evolve beyond your present state, which may be giving into your weaker state that keeps you stuck and trapped.

Put yourself out there. Take a chance and speak to strangers. Do the things you never tried. What do you have to lose? You see, one of the things that hold us back is in believing there is something to lose in taking a risk.

You are on a mission to engage in the total human experience by throwing it all on the line. Try the things that you are afraid of doing. You're not going to lose anything, I swear. You will only gain from it, even if you fail or are turned down.

Don't focus on the outcome. Drop your expectations. Expecting everything to work out is going to scare you into not doing anything. You'll suffer from **action paralysis**.

Here are some examples:

- You start up a YouTube channel to document your blogs or tell people how your week is going, make a mini-documentary out of it.

- You call up people that you would normally avoid.

- You talk openly with people about whatever is on your mind.

- You introduce yourself to random people at the supermarket.

- You tell your spouse and children you love them.

- You admit you are not perfect and you make mistakes.

- You try doing the one thing you swear you'd never do.

- You make it a daily habit to ask for at least one thing that you want.

Your conditioned response can be mastered through desensitizing and conditioning your mind to handle the bad stuff when it happens. You can, over time, condition your mind to adapt to getting told *NO*, "Get lost," "You're no good"; whatever people throw at you, you'll be ready to take it.

But the in the beginning it will be tough. Our fear of getting rejected is, like any fear, all-empowering until we strip it of all power it has over us. You have to prove to yourself the fear is a lie. You can instill in your confidence that all's right with the world and that you are going to get through this no matter what.

Here is an example. You have had an idea for a business that you want to start up. But you only think of it and never act on it. You're afraid of failing. What would it take for you to start up the one thing you have always feared doing? What would be the first step you could take? What would be the smallest initial step you could take?

We get overwhelmed when we think about all the big stuff. So, how about drilling down as small as you can? Not everything has to be taken in one big leap.

Think about where you'd be in six months from now and work toward a plan that produces real results. How would you feel in a few weeks if you suddenly took charge, put yourself out there, and started taking action on the fears that hold you back?

I can tell you this from experience: **Rejection would lose all its power over you.** In fact, you'd wonder what you were ever afraid of in the first place. But you have to start with something.

When you realize that rejection is less about you as a person and more to do with the request and dynamics of the situation, as well as how people are feeling at the moment, it becomes so much easier to just put yourself out there, it becomes easier to deal with.

It's just the way things are; we don't live in a perfect world. In a perfect world everyone gets along and gets what they want. In the real world, we know that isn't the case. In understanding this bitter pill of reality, we can look at our life problems and fears as less personal.

Toughen up and face the rejection that has been keeping you scared. For the most part, rejection is nothing more than an emotional response to a situation that you disapprove of or disapproves of you.

Action Plan: The 30-Day "Rejected on Purpose" Challenge

Here is what you are going to do. If you follow this system, within a few days and the weeks to come you are going to see that the rejection is only alive within you. It exists nowhere else. Nobody can reject you better than you can do it to yourself.

- Make a list of all the things you avoid because of your fear or anxiety around rejection.

- Now that you have your list, you're going to start doing these things.

- What would you do first if you knew that you couldn't be rejected?

A mentor of mine suggested this, and it was a miracle step. I had never done it before but after completing this simple action step, it was easy to look and see what I could actually do to overcome my rejected self. It was like a roadmap I had created, a checklist of sorts where I could go down the list and start checking things off as I did them.

Here is what you do:

Taking action toward the things that frighten you empowers your senses like nothing else. It pulls you out of that safety zone you have built to protect yourself. Your comfort zone is a cushion for survival. Sometimes we need the protection it offers; but most of the time we stay there and never make progress.

Just imagine how many opportunities you are going to create from today by doing the stuff that has always frightened you.

- Will you write a book?

- Will you publish a book?

- Start to interact with people more instead of shying away? (I am not referring to social media, but real interaction.)

- Take a job interview that you've been avoiding?

- Test-drive a sports car even if you don't have the money to buy it?

- Talk to someone that you've been avoiding?

Take action and take it every day. When you are fearful and believe you'll fail, do it anyway. Taking charge of your life is an action and not an event. You seize the day when you seize the moment. Nobody is giving you a roadmap to follow; the only map is the one you are creating today.

Will you live as a free individual?

Are you ready to be rejection free?

Action Plan

Take thirty minutes to come up with all the ways you can push yourself to take action toward something you normally wouldn't do. If your fear of rejection lies in relationships, you may have rejection issues with men or women. If your rejection issues are centered on acceptance, you might struggle to join in groups or events that center around community or social activities.

But there is a different variety to this game as well. In your daily life, make notes of all the opportunities you have to take a chance on something and you don't. You want to, but you hesitate because you are scared or you believe you'll fail.

Log these situations into your memory, and then try to challenge it. You may experience as I have that your rejection-centered self is controlled by fear in several situations. Once you identify what those situations are, you can then set up a strategy to take action in that area.

For example, I had a major fear of public speaking. I avoided it at all costs. So, I put myself in a situation where I had to give a speech and discuss something openly in public.

My other fear was meeting new people. With vulnerability issues, I made myself vulnerable. In the beginning I had a physical reaction to this approach with sweating and shaking. But after trying it ten times, I went from fear to desensitization of the rejection.

Try this and you will see it works. You can get the freedom to be yourself, and then, as you take more chances by putting yourself out there, you'll experience a new freedom you never had before. I remember having this feeling that the loneliness I carried with me every day was mostly my own making. Focusing on desensitizing strategies cured me of the pain of isolation.

For me that was the freedom I had always been after.

You can have that, too.

Building the Rejection Free Lifestyle

"I think that you have to believe in your destiny; that you will succeed, you will meet a lot of rejection and it is not always a straight path, there will be detours – so enjoy the view."

— **Michael York**

You can create your own lifestyle, experience a transformation, or make choices that take you in a completely new direction. You are as free as you want to be. By challenging the fear and doing what scares you, rejection no longer has any power over you. You can gain strength from the power of thought, confidence, and pushing your self-esteem to new levels.

Before we part ways, I want to leave you with three final lessons from this book. But before that, let me say that this is a fascinating journey we are on. What makes it so interesting is that we are given so many chances to live life as we want to.

Now, here are three final lessons...

Lesson #1: Tell Your Story

For a lot of years, I didn't think I had anything interesting to say. I was always afraid I'd be boring or people would dismiss my opinions or ideas as brining or unintellectual.

Then I became a good storyteller. I practiced telling stories in a way that engaged people. I did this not so that I could be more popular or get all the attention; I did it because I genuinely like people and want to share my own life lessons.

One of the biggest reasons for writing about rejection and sharing this experience with you is so that we can learn from each other's journey. Everyone has a story to tell, and it is essential that you get your story out there. You never know the impact you could have on one life.

Listen to the message that people are trying to get across. If you show a keen interest in someone they'll really open up and share their dreams and aspirations. This is the start of a good relationship.

Many relationships start off shallow and lacking any depth. People are afraid to get close or let down their guard. You can have the advantage by showing genuine interest and getting to know the other person through exchanging experiences.

Lesson #2: Put Your Flaws into Perspective

This is a book on self-improvement. With this material I hope that you have gained some benefit and can apply it to your life *right now*. Just take note that self-development doesn't mean self-perfection. We rejectees really beat up on ourselves. We ask ourselves for years, "What is wrong with me? Why am I so different?"

You are not so much different. It's just that everyone else is trying so hard to be normal that it just feels that way.

We all have flaws. It's okay. You've live with these flaws up until now, and that is okay too. With this book I hope that you can overcome and manage some of your flaws; other flaws we cannot change, or they may take more time to heal.

There is no big hurry. You have time. One day at a time and you'll make it. You can accept yourself as you are, flaws and golden points. You might feel awkward or ashamed. But what are your good points? What makes you unique and valuable? List these out and remind yourself what they are.

Lesson #3: Take Action Consistently

Nothing will happen to change your fears, and in turn your life, unless you make the changes. To do this you have to be focused on the changes you want to see happen in your life as the result of your choices.

Do you want to stay trapped or break free? Will you explore the unknowns of your real self, or stay hidden behind a veil of fear that keeps you doing the same thing over and over again? Will you take action or wait for action to be taken against you?

The key to creating lasting change is to do something repetitively over a long period of time. It is the same with building habits. Do something for a few weeks and you'll gain some momentum, but if you stop, the habit you are trying to replace will return. You can start to **transform your life today** by taking some small action daily. Ask for something you want; take a small risk; read a book on personal development.

Stay focused on your path to becoming *Rejection Free* and you'll soon find yourself living a new life in different ways.

I know you'll do what is best. Do it for yourself. Do what you've always wanted to do but lacked the courage to move forward. Know that you can do anything you want to do if you have the courage to take action

Assess where you are at in your life and take that first step forward. Just one step will do. For today.

Small steps are big gains over time.

Embrace the courage to ask for the things you want.

Help people get what they want.

Be who you are and not what the world thinks you should be.

You have a choice. Now go out there, seize the moment and live your life the way it was meant to be.

Life is too short to be scared. Defeat rejection and live the *Rejection Free* lifestyle.

I'll see you there…

Scott Allan

7 Tips for Handling Rejection Sensitivity

Rejection is about you, not them.

One of the greatest illusions about rejection is that we convince ourselves we are being personally "rejected," as if someone is doing something to us. But in fact, the rejection begins on the inside. This can be traced back to your inner critics, those old voices that tell you, "You're no good," or "Why bother? You'll just fail anyway."

When we reject ourselves first, we are sending a clear message to people. It is like putting the writing on the wall yourself. People can sense when someone is lacking confidence. If you walk into a bank to get a loan and you believe—even before you meet with the loans officer—that there's no way you'll get the loan, this feeling carries with you. Be aware of situations in which you're rejecting yourself before anyone else gets a chance to.

Stop blaming external forces for failed results.

Taking full responsibility for your life and current situation is a powerful character-building step. By taking charge, you take control. Deciding to stop blaming others for your unhappiness is taking a healthy approach to being responsible. This doesn't mean you have to forget what happened in the past, but you do have to move on from it.

This can only happen when you choose to live life on your terms by making a firm decision and following through with action to create a positive and fulfilling future. You are giving yourself permission to be free. Nobody else will give that to you. Once you accept your life as it is and are willing to do whatever it takes to move forward, then you are ready to be responsible.

Practice forgiveness, acceptance, and commit to moving forward. Don't stay stuck in one spot, waiting for someone else to make it all better. When you wait for someone else to take charge, you lose the chance to make the situation better and the opportunity to heal yourself is gone.

Take an opinion as a biased lack of knowledge.

Everyone has an opinion. It is one of the ways we communicate our thoughts and emotions. We formulate opinions about each other based on what is said, actions taken, or differences in personality. If you struggle with rejection, then varying opinions can have a negative impact on your confidence.

We take the opinions and judgments from others as a personal insult. If someone doesn't like the way you look or dress, or they don't like your attitude and the way you carry yourself, you may take this too personally. There are many details other people use to construct an opinion about you as a person.

It is easy to believe everything you hear, especially if you are hypersensitive. Even though we can't stop the world from having opinions, we can choose how to accept it. Will you retaliate and come back with your own attack? Or will you take what is said as a biased remark based on lack of evidence? Besides, who really knows you better than yourself? Why should you take someone else's word as the only truth when you know it just isn't so?

This works the other way, too. Your evaluation of another person is based on the same lack of information that others use to construct their opinions about you. You have two choices here: You can continue the negative cycle of labeling others just as they label you, or you can practice total acceptance as a strategy to build more empathy toward others.

A lack of empathy is at the core of many social problems. When we buy in to the opinions and criticisms of strangers, we believe what *they* decide is the truth about us. But it's not. Rarely are first opinions correct.

Revisit your shame-based childhood.

For most people, living in rejection has its roots in early childhood. Back then, we were treated without the attention or respect we deserved. Criticism was rampant. We were never good enough, no matter how hard we tried or what level of success we could achieve. This resulted in a life of living in shame, a core attribute of those who feel rejected.

It can be a painful experience to revisit this period of our lives when not everything was perfect. But by returning to that particular event in your past when you were most vulnerable, and by walking yourself through that pain again, in time you can mend the damage that was inflicted.

Let go of the past failures that define you.

If you were rejected in the past, you'll reject yourself in the future. We replay old stories of failures and negative results from our past. When this happens, we create more of the same. Your past is not who you are; it is who you were. Are you the same person you were twenty years ago? I know I'm not.

Sure, many things about you haven't changed and people still refer to you as someone they know based on a lifetime of friendship. But we are all evolving even if those changes are subtle. Basing your future happiness or success on what you got in the past is a way to repeat history. You can define your future by the actions you take now. Your thoughts, words, and emotions are powerful and can change your life in a moment if conditioned properly.

Practice getting rejected on purpose.

In his bestselling book, *Rejection Proof*, Jia Jiang takes on a massive challenge. He set out to get rejected over the course of 100 days in a project he dubbed 100 Days of Rejection.

During this social experiment, Jia would try outrageous stunts of courage to push his fear of rejection beyond anything he had ever experienced. He would ask for Olympic symbol donuts, give $5 to five random people, and challenge a CEO to a staring contest. His purpose was to desensitize himself to rejection so that he could overcome his fears in order to live his dream as an entrepreneur.

So, how about you? In what ways could you put yourself out there and get rejected in order to numb yourself to the fear? We put more effort into avoiding fear than encouraging it. So when rejection happens (and it will) it hurts and we remember the pain as something we'd rather not repeat. As a result, we stay away from it as much as possible.

Build your confidence through consistent practice.

The way to build confidence is to take action. Challenge yourself to do the things that are difficult. These are easy to spot because we resist what we don't want to do. Or we put off difficult tasks because they are hard but actually carry the greatest rewards in the long run.

Confidence is an "action building" activity. It can only be built when we put our fears and uncertainties to the test. You can use this list of Rejection Strategies as a starting point to develop a higher level of confidence and assurance.

Now, turn the page and join in the fun…your 30-day Rejection Free challenge!

Rejected on Purpose

YOUR 30-DAY REJECTION FREE CHECKLIST

Welcome to the Rejection Free Journey!

This is a checklist of 30 ways you can challenge the fear of rejection. Have fun by checking items off the list. Make a goal to tackle one challenge a day. Once you've completed the list, start making one of your own!

Some of these challenges are outrageous, but there is a purpose for taking direct action when you're scared, and that's to break you out of your comfort zone. Do what you're afraid to do, and do it as often as you can!

I see people taking off-the-wall actions every day, and my first thought is always that I wish I had the courage to do it, too. One day, I decided I wanted to have the courage to do the things I'm scared to do and to not let that fear hold me back. For most of us, the fear of rejection is so deeply embedded in our lives that it stops us from taking even the simplest of actions.

Why are we afraid?

We don't want to look foolish. Or needy. Or weak. What will people think? What if they laugh at me? What if I fail? What if I succeed? What if I can't handle being rejected? How will I survive?

When you put yourself out there and let people see the real you, it opens up a universe of vulnerability most of us have tried to keep closed.

There are **two massive fears** that keep you trapped. The first is the fear of people. Being judged, critiqued, or laughed at. To some degree, we go to great lengths to protect our ego. So we play it safe, stay low, and do what the world expects.

But…you can't step into greatness by doing what is best for everyone else.

Taking on this challenge, you'll discover that **other people are just like you.** They are also afraid. Everyone who looks so brave and courageous would love it if you walked up to them and asked for their opinion on something, or made their day with a huge smile and inquired, "How are you doing?"

Yes, you will be ignored by some. Strangers may turn away when you try to help them. But consider the other person might also be carrying fear or sorrow within them. How much fear is she walking around with? You become the fearless one when you reach out, approach someone else, and do what has been keeping you stuck.

Everyone else is afraid, too. Yes, it is hard to believe, but you are not the only one who thinks rejection is unique. We all believe that rejection has a stake in our lives. In many ways, everyone has their own struggle with rejection. People are afraid for many reasons, but those who can acknowledge it and defeat adversity will be ready for any challenge.

Another fear is related to how we perceive others as judging us. We fear failing, looking dumb, or being ridiculed. This fear runs deep and to avoid experiencing a frightening experience such as rejection, we do everything in our power to stay hidden. When this happens, we stop taking risks. We stop communicating or reaching out to people. We become suspicious of other people's intentions.

Breaking the Fear of Rejection

Taking a risk is like skating on a lake that has thin ice. The only difference is, we want the ice to break. That ice represents a level of your fear that you have to crack before you can feel comfortable.

Maybe you're afraid of public speaking, but you have to give a presentation. Or ask a favor of a stranger. Maybe you're a salesperson and you're afraid of being rejected by potential customers.

How do you bust that fear? By putting yourself in a position in which you have to skate on thin ice.

I hope you enjoy embracing the best parts of yourself, and keep working toward making the most out of your life. Don't let the fear hold you back. Embrace rejection as a learning platform, and think of it as an opportunity instead of a setback.

Before the Challenge

Record yourself—using audio, video, or both—as you answer the following questions: How are you feeling prior to the challenge, and how would you describe your level of fear? What thoughts are going through your mind?

It is very important that you make a recording of your answers to these questions. This is because you will need to compare the before and after results. Once you've done this, would you attempt the challenge again and expect better results?

By recording how you sound when you're experiencing fear, and how you overcome it by taking intentional action, you will become desensitized to the initial rejection. Can you imagine what you will do when you realize that you can do anything? The only thing holding you back is yourself, not some invisible force.

After the challenge

Record yourself afterward, too. How do you feel now? What were the reactions of the people you spoke with, if any? What could you have done differently to push the envelope?

There are only three rules.

Keep it legal. Don't do anything that goes beyond the bounds of the law. While I trust that you won't, it's important to note it here regardless.

Keep it fun. We take ourselves too seriously when we try to act like normal people, when in fact we're anything but that. Human beings are fun, spontaneous, and adventurous, with a gift for exploration. As you explore your fears, pushing your boundaries to new levels of unlimited potential, remember to breathe and enjoy life.

Keep it challenging. When we push beyond our comfort zone, we tend to experience fear. If you're not scared, you probably didn't leave your comfort zone. Challenge yourself at least once a day to keep pushing, interacting, and connecting with others. You may discover they're just as afraid of rejection as you are.

The time for living in fear is over.

Rejected on Purpose:
30 Point Challenge Checklist

Preparing for the challenge...

- Set a goal for yourself: How many challenges can you achieve in one year?

- You can include personal challenges not included on this list

- Record your experience with your camera or audio.

- Share it with your friends.

(1). Smile as big as you can and say, "Hello, how are you doing?" Do this with twenty people you don't know.

(2). If it's raining, offer your umbrella to someone who doesn't have one.

(3). Ask a stranger if you can interview them for ten minutes. Tell them you are practicing to be a life coach and would like to ask them several questions.

(4). In a restaurant, walk up to a random couple at a table and ask them if you can buy them each a glass of wine.

(5). Give away 50 candies on the street. You have to get rid of all of them.

(6). Shake someone's hand, and hold the shake for the duration of the conversation.

(7). Approach people at random and complement each of them. This can be about something they are wearing, their style of haircut, or a personal characteristic you noticed.

(8). When you're out walking, ask someone if they'd like to have a race to the end of the street.

(9). Walk up to 10 random people and ask if you can get your picture taken together. Make it a "selfie" moment.

(10). Walk into a car dealership and ask to take an expensive car for a test-drive.

(11). Reach out to a podcaster who has a popular show and ask if he or she would interview you.

(12). Deliver a presentation or webinar to a large audience of people or students on a topic you are not familiar with. Public speaking (also known as *glossophobia*) is an intense fear for many people. If you challenge this, it's a big win for you!

(13). Send your résumé *again* to a company that has already rejected you as an applicant.

(14). Go to a furniture store and ask if you can take a twenty-minute power nap on one of their model beds.

(15). Meet with your employer or boss at work and ask him or her if you can finish working thirty minutes earlier from now on to spend more time at home with family.

(16). Tell someone you have resentment against that you appreciate him or her being a part of your life.

(17). On an airplane, ask the cabin crew if they would give you a tour of the cockpit. Then, ask if you can interview the pilot.

(18). Enter a race or tournament. This could be tennis, karate, a marathon or something else that challenges you physically and mentally. Win or lose, just enter and do your best.

(19). Tell someone it's your birthday, and ask them to sing Happy Birthday to you.

(20). In a supermarket or café, ask if you can "skip to the front of the line" because you are "patience intolerant."

(21). Check in for a flight and ask to be upgraded to first class without paying extra.

(22). Ask someone who's eating ice cream if you can have some.

(23). Challenge someone to a staring contest. You have to hold the stare for a minimum of one minute.

(24). Sign up for an aerobics or yoga class and then, in one of the sessions, ask the instructor if *you* can lead the class today.

(25). Walk up to a complete stranger and start a conversation. Just start talking about anything. Ask them how their day is going. What is new in their life? What goals or aspirations do they have?

(26). Ask random people if they would like to play tic-tac-toe. The best 2/3 wins.

(27). Draw a picture. This can be anything. You can add color to it or make it as creative as you like. Then, carry it around for the day and whenever you meet someone, show them the drawing and ask, "So, what do you think?"

(28). Ask a random couple on the street to tell you the story of how they met.

(29). Write an article and submit to a magazine or online blog sites. Consider pitching your article to The Huffington Post or high-paying magazines.

(30). Ask someone for something that you really want. If they give you a NO, ask again on a different day. Or ask another person. The fear of asking stops most people from getting what they really want. Ask for it!

Unique Challenges

The last five rejection challenges are for you. This space is for you to come up with a plan to challenge your own fears. What are you going to do to become Rejection Free?

Unique challenge 1

Unique challenge 2

Unique challenge 3

Unique challenge 4

Unique challenge 5

Congratulations on taking the **Rejected on Purpose** challenge! Now that your confidence is at its peak, challenge yourself to try one new challenge every week. Keep pushing forward to break your fear and desensitize your rejection fears.

About Scott Allan

Scott Allan is a bestselling author who has a passion for teaching, building life skills, and inspiring others to take charge of their lives.

Scott's mission is to give people the strategies needed to design the life they want through choice.

He believes successful living is a series of small, consistent actions taken every day to build a thriving lifestyle with intentional purpose.

By taking the necessary steps and eliminating unwanted distractions that keep you stuck, you are free to focus on the essentials.

You can connect with Scott online at:

Blog: www.scottallanauthor.com

Amazon Books: amazon.com/author/scottallan

Books by Scott Allan

Check out these other bestselling books by Scott Allan. You can visit his website at **www.scottallanauthor.com** to stay up to date on all future book releases, or amazon.com/author/scottallan

Empower Your Thoughts: Control Worry and Anxiety, Develop a Positive Mental Attitude, and Master Your Mindset

Empower Your Fear: Leverage Your Fears To Rise Above Mediocrity and Turn Self-Doubt Into a Confident Plan of Action

Empower Your Success: Success Strategies to Maximize Performance, Take Positive Action, and Engage Your Enthusiasm for Living a Great Life

Rejection Reset: A Strategic Step-By-Step Program for Restoring Self-Confidence, Reshaping an Inferior Mindset, and Thriving In a Shame-Free Lifestyle

Rejection Free: How To Choose Yourself First and Take Charge of Your Life By Confidently Asking For What You Want

Do It Scared: Charge Forward With Confidence, Conquer Resistance, and Break Through Your Limitations

Relaunch Your Life: Break the Cycle of Self-Defeat, Destroy Negative Emotions, and Reclaim Your Personal Power

Drive Your Destiny: Create a Vision for Your Life, Build Better Habits for Wealth and Health, and Unlock Your Inner Greatness

The Discipline of Masters: Destroy Big Obstacles, Master Your Time, Capture Creative Ideas and Become the Leader You Were Born to Be

The Master of Achievement: Conquer Fear and Adversity, Maximize Big Goals, Supercharge Your Success and Develop a Purpose Driven Mindset

Undefeated: Persevere in the Face of Adversity, Master the Art of Never Giving Up, and Always Beat the Odds Stacked Against You

Fail Big: Fail Your Way to Success and Break All the Rules to Get There

Lifestyle Mastery Series: Vol 1: Books 1—3: Drive Your Destiny, The Discipline of Masters, and The Master of Achievement

Now you can listen to the audiobook version of **Rejection Free for Life** on Audible.

Visit Scott Allan online at:

https://scottallanauthor.com

Printed in Great Britain
by Amazon

77328697R00160